LAST
POETIC GEMS

SELECTED FROM THE WORKS

OF

WILLIAM McGONAGALL

Poet and Tragedian

Died in Edinburgh, 29th September 1902

Edited by
James L. Smith

DUNDEE:
DAVID WINTER & SON LTD.
15 SHORE TERRACE

1974

''A Summary History of Poet McGonagall'' and '' Requisition to the Queen '' are reproduced by kind permission of the Corporation of Dundee and are copyright

CONTENTS

CONTENTS

A SUMMARY HISTORY OF POET McGONAGALL

Poet McGonagall was born In the Month of March 1825. His parents were Irish and his Father left Ireland, shortly after His marriage and came to Scotland. And got settled down In Ayrshire In a place call'd Maybole as a Cotton Weaver, and lived there for About ten years untill the Cotton Weaving began to fail there, and Then he was Induced to leave it owing to the very small demand There was for Cotton weaving In that part of Scotland. Then he and his family left Maybole, and came to Edinburgh Where he got settled down again to work Cotton fabrics which there was a greater demand for, than in Maybole. and by this time they family consisted of two Sons, And three daughters. William, The Poet, was the youngest, and was born in Edinburgh. And the rest of the family was born in Maybole And Dundee. his Father lived in Edinburgh for more than eight years, untill the Cotton Weaving began to fail, then his Father and they family left Edinburgh, And travelled to the Orkney Isles, And to a house for they family to live in the Island of Southronaldsay And his father bought the Living as a Pedlar, and supported the family by selling hardware, among they peasantry In the Orkney Isles, and returning home every night to his family, when circumstances would permit him. Charles the eldest son was herding Cows to a Farmer in the Island of South-ronaldsay, and his eldest Sister Nancy, was in the service of a Farmer in the same locality, and William, the Poet, and Thomas, the second eldest brother, was sent to School to be teached by Mr. James Forbes, the parish Schoolmaster, Who was a very Strict Dominie indeed, of which our readers shall hear of as a proof of his strictness, a rather curious incident. William, the Poet, chanced to be one day in his garden behind the school, and Chanc'd to espy a live, Tortoise, that the Dominie kept in the garden. and never having seen such a curious kind of a reptile before, his Curiousity was therefore excited no doubt to see it, and he stooped down and lifted the Tortoise with both hands, thereon admiring the varied beautiful Colours of its shell. when behold it dunged upon both hands of William the poet, which was rather aggravating to William, no doubt, and he dash'd the Tortoise on the ground which almost killed it. And the Dominie Chanc'd to see him, at the time through the back window of the Schoolroom, and he rattled on the window with his Cane to William, which startled him, and as soon as William came in to the School, he layd hold of him and began to beat him unmercifully about the body and face, untill his face was blackened in many places, with his hard Taws. and persisted in it untill some of the elder Scholars cried out to him to Stop! beating William. and when William went home to his dinner, and told his kind father all about it as it had happened his father flew into a rage and said he would be revenged upon him for beating William so unmerciful, and accordingly he went to a Magistrate, with William, and related the Case to him as it had happened. and when the Magistrate examined Williams face, and seen the marks, the Dominie had left thereon he ask'd Williams father if he was willing to put him from ever being a Schoolmaster in the parish again, but Williams Father would not consent to hear of that owing to the Kindness he had shown towards his Son, Thomas, and he simply ask'd the Magistrate, to give him a line, to certify, to Mr. Forbes, that he could put him from ever being a Schoolmaster in that parish again if he would just say the word. so Williams Father went with him to the Dominie, and showed him the line he had got from the Magistrate, to certify that he could put him from being a Schoolmaster again in the parish if he would say the word. and when the Dominie read he was very much surprised and began to make an Apology to Williams Father for what he had done, and promised he would never do the like again. so William and his Father were well satisfied for getting such a sweet revenge, upon that Dominie, and ever after that William was a great favourite of the Dominies and just acted as he pleased and was always very unwilling to go to School. Williams Father had to beat him very often before he would go to School, so that he never got a very great share of education.

William has been like the Immortal Shakspeare he had learn'd more from nature than ever he learn'd at School. William has been from his Boyhood a great admirer of every thing that is Considered to be beautiful sush as beautiful Rivers and mountain Scenery and beautiful landscapes, and great men such as Shakspeare and great preachers, such as the Rev. George Gilfillan, and Great Poets such as Burns, or Tannahill, and Campbell &c. but again I must return to Williams Father he stay'd in the Island of Southronaldsay for about three years, and then left it with the Family, and came to Dundee, and settled down in it. and those of the family that were able to work were sent to the Mills and some of his Sons wrought at the handloom in the Factory along with himself, that was Thomas, and Charles, and William wrought in the Mill for a few years. and then his Father took him from the Mill, and learnd him the handloom himself and he has followed that occupation up to the present when he Can get it to do. he has always had a great liking for Theatrical representation and has made several appearances upon the Stage, In the Theatre Royal Dundee, In the Character of Macbeth, under

7

the Management of Mr. Caple. he has also play'd the Characters of Hamlet and Othello, Macbeth, and Richard III, In the Music Hall under the Management of Forrest Knowles, to delighted and crowded audiences. and it is only recently ago that he discovered himself to be a poet. the desire for writing Poetry came upon him In the Month of June 1877 that he could not resist the desire for writing poetry the first piece he wrote was An address to the Rev. George Gilfillan, to the Weekly News, only giving the Initials of his name, W. M. G. Dundee which was received with eclat, then he turned his muse to the Tay Bridge, and sung it successfully and was pronounced by the press the Poet Laurete of The Tay Bridge then he unfolded himself to they public, and honestly gave out to them his own name. then he wrote an Address to Robert Burns. Also upon Shakspeare, which he sent printed Copies of to her Majesty, and received her Royal Patronage for so doing. he has also Composed the following effusions, the Bonnie broon haird Lassie o' Bonnie Dundee, and A Companion to it Little Jeemie, also the Convicts return home again to Scotland and the Silvery Tay, and a host of others to numerous to mention, which will be publish'd shortly.

ⓒ *The Corporation of Dundee*

8

A REQUISITION TO THE QUEEN

Smiths Buildings No. 19
Patons Lane,
Dundee.
Sept the 6th. 1877.

1. Most August! Empress of India, and of great Britain the
   Queen,
   I most humbly beg your pardon, hoping you will not
   think it mean
   That a poor poet that lives in Dundee,
   Would be so presumptous to write unto Thee

2. Most lovely Empress of India, and Englands generous
   Queen,
   I send you an Address, I have written on Scotlands Bard,
   Hoping that you will accept it, and not be with me to
   hard,
   Nor fly into a rage, but be as Kind and Condescending
   As to give me your Patronage

3. Beautiful Empress, of India, and Englands Gracious
   Queen,
   I send you a Shakespearian Address written by me.
   And I think if your Majesty reads it, right pleased you
   will be.
   And my heart it will leap with joy, if it is patronized by
   Thee.

4. Most Mighty Empress, of India, and Englands beloved
   Queen,
   Most Handsome to be Seen.
   I wish you every Success.
   And that heaven may you bless.

9

For your Kindness to the poor while they are in distress.
I hope the Lord will protect you while living
    And hereafter when your Majesty is . . . dead.
I hope Thee Lord above will place an eternal Crown!
    upon your Head.
    I am your Gracious Majesty ever faithful to Thee,
William McGonagall, The Poor Poet,
    That lives in Dundee.

A NOTE ON THE TEXT

'A Summary History of Poet McGonagall' and 'A Requisition to the Queen' are printed exactly as they appear in McGonagall's handwriting in the Dundee Public Library, by whose courtesy they are here reproduced. The remaining poems are printed from the earliest broadsheets and newspapers, and are transcribed without correction to preserve as far as possible the poet's original grammar, spelling and punctuation.

—Ed.

McGONAGALL

THE DEMON DRINK

Oh, thou demon Drink, thou fell destroyer;
Thou curse of society, and its greatest annoyer.
What hast thou done to society, let me think ?
I answer thou hast caused the most of ills, thou demon
   Drink.

Thou causeth the mother to neglect her child,
Also the father to act as he were wild,
So that he neglects his loving wife and family dear,
By spending his earnings foolishly on whisky, rum, and beer.

And after spending his earnings foolishly he beats his wife—
The man that promised to protect her during life—
And so the man would if there was no drink in society,
For seldom a man beats his wife in a state of sobriety.

And if he does, perhaps he finds his wife fou',
Then that causes, no doubt, a great hullaballoo ;
When he finds his wife drunk he begins to frown,
And in a fury of passion he knocks her down.

And in the knock down she fractures her head,
And perhaps the poor wife is killed dead,
Whereas, if there was no strong drink to be got,
To be killed wouldn't have been the poor wife's lot.

Then the unfortunate husband is arrested and cast into jail,
And sadly his fate he does bewail ;
And he curses the hour that ever he was born,
And paces his cell up and down very forlorn.

11

And when the day of his trial draws near,
No doubt for the murdering of his wife he drops a tear,
And he exclaims, "Oh, thou demon Drink, through thee I
    must die,"
And on the scaffold he warns the people from drink to fly,

Because whenever a father or a mother takes to drink,
Step by step on in crime they do sink,
Until their children loses all affection for them,
And in justice we cannot their children condemn.

The man that gets drunk is little else than a fool,
And is in the habit, no doubt, of advocating for Home Rule ;
But the best Home Rule for him, as far as I can understand,
Is the abolition of strong drink from the land.

And the men that get drunk in general wants Home Rule ;
But such men, I rather think, should keep their heads cool,
And try and learn more sense, I most earnestly do pray,
And help to get strong drink abolished without delay.

If drink was abolished how many peaceful homes would
    there be,
Just, for instance, in the beautiful town of Dundee ;
Then this world would be a heaven, whereas it's a hell,
And the people would have more peace in it to dwell.

Alas ! strong drink makes men and women fanatics,
And helps to fill our prisons and lunatics ;
And if there was no strong drink such cases wouldn't be,
Which would be a very glad sight for all Christians to see.

I admit, a man may be a very good man,
But in my opinion he cannot be a true Christian
As long as he partakes of strong drink,
The more that he may differently think.

But, no matter what he thinks, I say nay,
For by taking it he helps to lead his brother astray,
Whereas, if he didn't drink, he would help to reform society,
And we would soon do away with all inebriety.

Then, for the sake of society and the Church of God,
Let each one try to abolish it at home and abroad;
Then poverty and crime would decrease and be at a stand,
And Christ's Kingdom would soon be established throughout
    the land.

Therefore, brothers and sisters, pause and think,
And try to abolish the foul fiend, Drink.
Let such doctrine be taught in church and school,
That the abolition of strong drink is the only Home Rule.

GRIF, OF THE BLOODY HAND

In an immense wood in the south of Kent,
There lived a band of robbers which caused the people
    discontent;
And the place they infested was called the Weald,
Where they robbed wayside travellers and left them dead on
    the field.

Their leader was called Grif, of the Bloody Hand,
And so well skilled in sword practice there's few could him
 withstand;
And sometimes they robbed villages when nothing else
 could be gained,
In the year of 1336, when King Edward the III. reigned.

The dress the robbers wore was deep coloured black,
And in courage and evil deeds they didn't lack;
And Grif, of the Bloody Hand, called them his devils,
Because they were ever ready to perform all kinds of ills.

'Twas towards the close of a very stormy day,
A stranger walked through the wood in search of Grif,
 without dismay;
And as the daylight faded he quickened his pace and ran,
Never suspecting that in his rear he was followed by a man.

And as the man to the stranger drew near,
He demanded in a gruff voice, what seek you here;
And when the stranger saw him he trembled with fear,
Because upon his head he wore a steel helmet, and in his
 hand he bore a spear.

What seek you here repeated the dark habited man,
Come, sir, speak out, and answer me if you can;
Are you then one of the devils demanded the stranger
 faintly,
That I am said the man, now what matters that to thee.

Then repeated the stranger, sir, you have put me to a stand,
But if I guess aright, you are Grif, of the Bloody Hand;
That I am replied Grif, and to confess it I'm not afraid,
Oh! well then I require your service and you'll be well paid.

14

But first I must know thy name, I, that's the point,
Then you shall have the help of my band conjoint;
Before any of my men on your mission goes,
Well then replied the stranger call me Martin Dubois.

Well sir, come tell me what you want as quick as you can,
Well then replied Dubois do you know one Halbert Evesham
That dwells in the little village of Brenchley,
Who has a foster child called Violet Evesham of rare beauty.

And you seek my aid to carry her off,
Ha! ha! a love affair, nay do not think I scoff;
For you shall enjoy her sir before this time to morrow,
If that will satisfy you, or help to drown your sorrow.

And now sir what is your terms with me,
Before I carry off Violet Evesham from the village of
    Brenchley;
Well Grif, one thousand marks shall be the pay,
'Tis agreed then cried Grif, and you shall enjoy her without
    delay.

Then the bargains struck, uttered Grif, how many men will
    you require,
Come sir, speak, you can have all my band if you desire;
Oh, thanks sir, replied Dubois, I consider four men will do,
That's to say sir if the four men's courage be true.

And to-morrow sir send the men to Brenchley without delay,
And remember one thousand merks will be the pay;
And the plan I propose is to carry her to the wood,
And I will be there to receive her, the plan is good.

And on the next morning Grif, of the Bloody Hand,
Told off four of his best men and gave them strict command;
To carry off Violet Evesham from the village of Brenchley,
And to go about it fearlessly and make no delay.

And when ye have captured her carry her to the wood,
Now remember men I wish my injunctions to be understood;
All right, captain, we'll do as we've be told,
And carry her off all right for the sake of the gold.

So on the next morning before the villagers were out of bed,
The four robbers marched into the village of Brenchley
    without any dread;
And boldly entered Violet Evesham's house and carried her,
    away,
While loudly the beautiful girl shrieked in dismay.

But when her old father missed her through the village he
    ran,
And roused the villagers to a man;
And a great number of them gathered, and Wat Tyler at
    their head,
And all armed to the teeth, and towards the wood they
    quickly sped.

And once within the wood Wat Tyler cried, where is Violet
    Evesham,
Then Grif, of the Bloody Hand cried, what ails the man;
My dear sir I assure you that Violet Evesham is not here.
Therefore good people I advise ye to retire from here.

No! I'll not back cried Wat Tyler, until I rescue Violet
    Evesham,
Therefore liar, and devil, defend thyself if you can;
Ay replied Grif, that I will thou braggart loon,
And with my sword you silly boy prepare for thy doom.

Then they rained their blows on each other as thick as hail,
Until at last Grif's strength began to fail;
Then Wat leaped upon him and threw him to the ground,
Then his men fled into the wood that were standing around.

Then the villagers shouted hurrah for Wat Tyler and
    victory,
And to search for Violet Evesham they willingly did agree;
And they searched the wood and found her at the foot of a
    tree,
And when she was taken home the villagers danced with
    glee.

And 'tis said Wat Tyler married Violet Evesham,
And there was great rejoicing among the villagers at the
    marriage so grand;
And Wat Tyler captured Dubois, and bound him to a tree,
And left him there struggling hard to gain his liberty.

A SUMMARY HISTORY OF LORD CLIVE

About a hundred and fifty years ago,
History relates it happened so,
A big ship sailed from the shores of Britain
Bound for India across the raging main.

And many of the passengers did cry and moan
As they took the last look of their old home,
Which they were fast leaving far behind,
And which some of them would long bear in mind.

Among the passengers was a youth about seventeen years
old,
Who had been a wild boy at home and very bold,
And by his conduct had filled his parents' hearts with woe,
Because to school he often refused to go.

And now that he was going so far away from home,
The thought thereof made him sigh and groan,
For he felt very sad and dejected were his looks,
And he often wished he had spent more time at his books.

And when he arrived in India he searched for work there,
And got to be clerk in a merchant's office, but for it he didn't
care;
The only pleasure he found was in reading books,
And while doing so, sad and forlorn were his looks.

One day while feeling unhappy he fired a pistol at his own
head,
Expecting that he would kill himself dead;
But the pistol wouldn't go off although he tried every plan,
And he felt sorry, and resolved to become a better man.

So Clive left his desk and became a soldier brave,
And soon rose to be a captain and manfully did behave;
For he beat the French in every battle,
After all their foolish talk and prattle.

Then he thought he would take a voyage home to his friends,
And for his bad behaviour towards them he would make
   some amends;
For he hadn't seen them for many years,
And when he thought of them he shed briny tears.

And when he arrived in London
The people after him in crowds did run;
And they flocked to see him every minute,
Because they thought him the most famous man in it.

And all the greatest people in the land
Were proud to shake him by the hand;
And they gave him a beautiful sword because he had fought
   so well
And of his bravery the people to each other did tell.

And when his own friends saw him they to him ran,
And they hardly knew him, he looked so noble a man;
And his parents felt o'erjoyed when they saw him home
   again,
And when he left his parents again for India it caused them
   great pain.

But it was a good thing Clive returned to India again,
Because a wicked prince in his territory wouldn't allow the
   British to remain,
And he resolved to drive them off his land,
And marched upon them boldly with thousands of his band

But the bad prince trembled when he heard that Clive had
    come,
Because the British at the charge of the bayonet made his
    army run;
And the bad prince was killed by one of his own band,
And the British fortunately got all his land.

And nearly all India now belongs to this country,
Which has been captured by land and by sea,
By some of the greatest men that ever did live,
But the greatest of them all was Robert Clive.

THE BATTLE OF THE NILE

'Twas on the 18th of August in the year of 1798,
That Nelson saw with inexpressible delight
The City of Alexandria crowded with the ships of France,
So he ordered all sail to be set, and immediately advance.

And upon the deck, in deep anxiety he stood,
And from anxiety of mind he took but little food;
But now he ordered dinner to be prepared without delay,
Saying, I shall gain a peerage to-morrow, or Westminster
    Abbey.

The French had found it impossible to enter the port of
    Alexandria,
Therefore they were compelled to withdraw;
Yet their hearts were burning with anxiety the war to begin,
But they couldn't find a pilot who would convey them
    safely in.

Therefore Admiral Brueys was forced to anchor in Aboukir
  Bay,
And in a compact line of battle, the leading vessel lay
Close to a shoal, along a line of very deep water,
There they lay, all eager to begin the murderous slaughter.

The French force consisted of thirteen ships of the line,
As fine as ever sailed on the salt sea brine;
Besides four Frigates carrying 1,196 guns in all,
Also 11,230 men as good as ever fired a cannon ball.

The number of the English ships were thirteen in all,
And carrying 1012 guns, including great and small;
And the number of the men were 8,068,
All jolly British tars and eager for to fight.

As soon as Nelson perceived the position of the enemy,
His active mind soon formed a plan immediately;
As the plan he thought best, as far as he could see,
Was to anchor his ships on the quarter of each of the enemy.

And when he had explained his mode of attack to his officers
  and men,
He said, form as convenient, and anchor at the stern;
Then first gain the victory, and make the best use of it you
  can,
Therefore I hope every one here to-day, will do their duty to
  a man.

When Captain Berry perceived the boldness of the plan,
He said, my Lord, I'm sure the men will do their duty to a
  man;
And, my Lord, what will the world say, if we gain the
  victory ?
Then Nelson replied, there's no if in the case, and that you'll
  see.

Then the British tars went to work without delay,
All hurrying to and fro, making ready for the fray;
And there wasn't a man among them, but was confident
   that day,
That they would make the French to fly from Aboukir Bay.

Nelson's Fleet did not enter Aboukir Bay at once,
And by adopting that plan, that was his only chance;
But one after another, they bore down on the enemy;
Then Nelson cried, now open fire my heroes, immediately!

Then the shores of Egypt trembled with the din of the war,
While sheets of flame rent the thick clouds afar;
And the contending fleets hung incumbent o'er the bay,
Whilst our British tars stuck to their guns without the least
   dismay.

And loudly roared the earthly thunder along the river Nile,
And the British ship Orion went into action in splendid
   style;
Also Nelson's Ship Vanguard bore down on the foe,
With six flags flying from her rigging high and low.

Then she opened a tremendous fire on the Spartiate,
And Nelson cried, fear not my lads we'll soon make them
   retreat!
But so terrific was the fire of the enemy on them,
That six of the Vanguards guns were cleared of men.

Yet there stood Nelson, the noble Hero of the Nile,
In the midst of death and destruction on deck all the while;
And around him on every side, the cannon balls did rattle,
But right well the noble hero knew the issue of the battle.

But suddenly he received a wound on the head,
And fell into the arms of Captain Berry, but fortunately not
   dead;
And the flow of blood from his head was very great,
But still the hero of the Nile was resigned to his fate.

Then to the Cockpit the great Admiral was carried down,
And in the midst of the dying, he never once did frown;
Nor he did'nt shake with fear, nor yet did he mourne,
But patiently sat down to wait his own turn.

And when the Surgeon saw him, he instantly ran,
But Nelson said, Surgeon, attend to that man;
Attend to the sailor you were at, for he requires your aid,
Then I will take my turn, don't be the least afraid.

And when his turn came, it was found that his wound was
   but slight,
And when known, it filled the sailors hearts with delight;
And they all hoped he would soon be able to command in the
   fight,
When suddenly a cry arose of fire! which startled Nelson
   with affright.

And unassisted he rushed upon the deck, and to his amaze,
He discovered that the Orient was all in a blaze;
Then he ordered the men to lower the boats, and relieve the
   enemy,
Saying, now men, see and obey my orders immediately.

Then the noble tars manned their boats, and steered to the
    Orient,
While the poor creatures thanked God for the succour He
    had sent;
And the burning fragments fell around them like rain,
Still our British tars rescued about seventy of them from the
    burning flame,

And of the thirteen sail of the French the British captured
    nine,
Besides four of their ships were burnt, which made the scene
    sublime,
Which made the hero of the Nile cry out thank God we've
    won the day,
And defeated the French most manfully in Aboukir Bay.

Then the victory was complete and the French Fleet
    annihilated,
And when the news arrived in England the peoples' hearts
    felt elated,
Then Nelson sent orders immediately through the fleet,
That thanksgiving should be returned to God for the victory
    complete.

BEAUTIFUL ABERFOYLE

The mountains and glens of Aberfoyle are beautiful to sight,
Likewise the rivers and lakes are sparkling and bright;
And its woods were frequented by the Lady of the Lake,
And on its Lakes many a sail in her boat she did take.

The scenery there will fill the tourist with joy,
Because 'tis there once lived the bold Rob Roy,
Who spent many happy days with his Helen there,
By chasing the deer in the woods so fair.

The little vale of Aberfoyle and its beautiful river
Is a sight, once seen, forget it you'll never;
And romantic ranges of rock on either side
Form a magnificent background far and wide.

And the numerous lochs there abound with trout
Which can be had for the taking out,
Especially from the Lochs Chon and Ard,
There the angler can make a catch which will his toil reward.

And between the two lochs the Glasgow Water Works are
    near,
Which convey water of Loch Katrine in copious streams
    clear
To the inhabitants of the Great Metropolis of the West,
And for such pure water they should think themselves blest.

The oak and birch woods there are beautiful to view,
Also the Ochil hills which are blue in hue,
Likewise the Lake of Menteith can be seen far eastward,
Also Stirling Castle, which long ago the English besieged
    very hard.

Then away to Aberfoyle, Rob Roy's country,
And gaze on the magnificent scenery.
A region of rivers and mountains towering majestically
Which is lovely and fascinating to see.

But no words can describe the beautiful scenery.
Aberfoyle must be visited in order to see,
So that the mind may apprehend its beauties around,
Which will charm the hearts of the visitors I'll be bound.

As for the clachan of Aberfoyle, little remains but a hotel,
Which for accommodation will suit the traveller very well.
And the bedding there is clean and good,
And good cooks there to cook the food.

Then away to the mountains and lakes of bonnie Aberfoyle,
Ye hard-working sons and daughters of daily toil;
And traverse its heathery mountains and view its lakes so
    clear,
When the face of Nature's green in the spring of the year.

THE CONVICT'S RETURN

Ye mountains and glens of fair Scotland I'm with ye once
    again,
During my absence from ye my heart was like to break in
    twain;
Oh! how I longed to see you and the old folks at home,
And with my lovely Jeannie once more in the green woods
    to roam.

Now since I've returned safe home again
I will try and be content
With my lovely Jeannie at home,
And forget my banishment.

My Jeannie and me will get married,
And I will be to her a good man,
And we'll live happy together,
And do the best we can.

I hope my Jeannie and me
Will always happy be,
And never feel discontent;
And at night at the fireside
I'll relate to her the trials of my banishment.

But now I will never leave my Jeannie again
Until the day I die;
And before the vital spark has fled
I will bid ye all good-bye.

THE BATTLE OF ALEXANDRIA, OR
THE RECONQUEST OF EGYPT

It was on the 21st of March in the year of 1801,
The British were at their posts every man;
And their position was naturally very strong,
And the whole line from sea to lake was about a mile long.

And on the ruins of a Roman Palace, rested the right,
And every man amongst them was eager for the fight,
And the reserve was under the command of Major General
    Moore,
A hero brave, whose courage was both firm and sure.

27

And in the valley between the right were the cavalry,
Which was really a most beautiful sight to see;
And the 28th were posted in a redoubt open in the rear,
Determined to hold it to the last without the least fear.

And the Guards and the Inniskillings were eager for the fray,
Also the Gordon Highlanders and Cameron Highlanders in
    grand array;
Likewise the dismounted Cavalry and the noble Dragoons,
Who never fear'd the cannons shot when it loudly booms.

And between the two armies stretched a sandy plain,
Which the French tried to chase the British off, but it was
    all in vain,
And a more imposing battle-field seldom has been chosen,
But alack the valour of the French soon got frozen.

Major General Moore was the general officer of the night,
And had galloped off to the left and to the right,
The instant he heard the enemy briskly firing;
He guessed by their firing they had no thought of retiring.

Then a wild broken huzza was heard from the plain below,
And followed by a rattle of musketry from the foe;
Then the French advanced in column with their drums
    loudly beating,
While their officers cried forward men and no retreating.

Then the colonel of the 58th reserved his fire,
Until the enemy drew near, which was his desire;
Then he ordered his men to attack them from behind the
    palace wall,
Then he opened fire at thirty yards, which did the enemy
    appal.

And thus assailed in front, flank, and rear,
The French soon began to shake with fear;
Then the 58th charged them with the bayonet, with courage
  unshaken,
And all the enemy that entered the palace ruins were killed
  or taken.

Then the French Invincibles, stimulated by liquor and the
  promise of gold,
Stole silently along the valley with tact and courage bold,
Proceeded by a 6 pounder gun, between the right of the
  guards,
But brave Lieutenant-Colonel Stewart quickly their
  progress retards.

Then Colonel Stewart cried to the right wing,
Forward! my lads, and make the valley ring,
And charge them with your bayonets and capture their gun,
And before very long they will be glad to run.

Then loudly grew the din of battle, like to rend the skies,
As Major Stirling's left wing faced, and charged them
  likewise;
Then the Invincibles maddened by this double attack,
Dashed forward on the palace ruins, but they soon were
  driven back.

And by the 58th, and Black Watch they were brought to
  bay, here,
But still they were resolved to sell their lives most dear,
And it was only after 650 of them had fallen in the fray,
That the rest threw down their arms and quickly ran away.

Then unexpected, another great body of the enemy was seen,
With their banners waving in the breeze, most beautiful and
green;
And advancing on the left of the redoubt,
But General Moore instantly ordered the Black Watch out.

And he cried, brave Highlanders you are always in the
hottest of the fight,
Now make ready for the bayonet charge with all your might;
And remember our country and your forefathers
As soon as the enemy and ye foregathers.

Then the Black Watch responded with a loud shout,
And charged them with their bayonets without fear or
doubt;
And the French tried hard to stand the charge, but it was all
in vain,
And in confussion they all fled across the sandy plain.

Oh! it was a glorious victory, the British gained that day,
But the joy of it, alas! was unfortunately taken away,
Because Sir Ralph Abercrombie, in the hottest of the fight,
was shot,
And for his undaunted bravery, his name will never be
forgot.

SAVED BY MUSIC

At one time, in America, many years ago,
Large gray wolves wont to wander to and fro;
And from the farm yards they carried pigs and calves away,
Which they devoured ravenously, without dismay.

But, as the story goes, there was a negro fiddler called old
   Dick,
Who was invited by a wedding party to give them music,
In the winter time, when the snow lay thick upon the ground,
And the rivers far and near were frozen all around.

So away went Dick to the wedding as fast as he could go,
Walking cautiously along o'er the crisp and crackling snow,
And the path was a narrow one, the greater part of the way
Through a dark forest, which filled his heart with dismay.

And when hurrying onward, not to be late at the festival,
He heard the howl of a wolf, which did his heart appal,
And the howl was answered, and as the howl came near
Poor Old Dick, fiddle in hand, began to shake with fear.

And as the wolves gathered in packs from far and near,
Old Dick in the crackling bushes did them hear,
And they ran along to keep pace with him,
Then poor Dick began to see the danger he was in.

And every few minutes a wolf would rush past him with a
   snap,
With a snapping sound like the ring of a steel trap,
And the pack of wolves gathered with terrible rapidity,
So that Dick didn't know whether to stand or flee.

And his only chance, he thought, was to keep them at bay
By preserving the greatest steadiness without dismay,
Until he was out of the forest and on open ground,
Where he thought a place of safety might be found.

31

He remembered an old hut stood in the clearing,
And towards it he was slowly nearing,
And the hope of reaching it urged him on,
But he felt a trifle dispirited and woe-begone.

And the poor fellow's heart with fear gave a bound,
When he saw the wolves' green eyes glaring all around,
And they rushed at him boldly, one after another,
Snapping as they passed, which to him was great bother.

And Dick sounded his fiddle and tried to turn them back,
And the sound caused the wolves to leap back in a crack,
When Dick took to his heels at full run,
But now poor Dick's danger was only begun :

For the wolves pursued him without delay,
But Dick arrived at the hut in great dismay,
And had just time to get on the roof and play,
And at the strains of the music the wolves felt gay.

And for several hours he sat there in pain,
Knowing if he stopped playing the wolves would be at him
    again,
But the rage of the wolves abated to the subduing strains,
And at last he was rewarded for all his pains :

For the wedding-party began to weary for some music,
And they all came out to look for Old Dick,
And on the top of the hut they found him fiddling away,
And they released him from his dangerous position without
    delay.

BEAUTIFUL NEWPORT ON THE BRAES
O' THE SILVERY TAY

Bonnie Mary, the Maid o' the Tay,
Come! let's go, and have a holiday
In Newport, on the braes o' the silvery Tay,
'Twill help to drive dull care away.

The scenery there is most enchanting to be seen,
Especially the fine mansions with their shrubbery green;
And the trees and ivy are beautiful to view
Growing in front of each stately home in the avenue.

There the little birds and beautiful butterflies
Are soaring heavenwards almost to the skies,
And the busy bees are to be seen on the wing,
As from flower to flower they hummingly sing,

As they gather honey all the day,
From the flowery gardens of Newport on the braes o' the
    Tay.
And as we view the gardens our hearts will feel gay
After being pent up in the workshop all the day.

Then there's a beautiful spot near an old mill,
Suitable for an artist to paint of great skill,
And the trees are arched o'erhead, lovely to be seen,
Which screens ye from the sunshine's glittering sheen.

Therefore, holiday makers, I'd have ye resort
To Newport on the braes o' the Tay for sport,
And inhale the pure air with its sweet perfume,
Emanating from the flowery gardens of Newport and the
    yellow broom.

And when bright Sol sinks in the West
You'll return home at night quite refreshed,
And dream in your beds of your rambles during the day
Along the bonnie braes o' the silvery Tay.

THE BATTLE OF CORUNNA

'Twas in the year of 1808, and in the autumn of the year,
Napoleon resolved to crush Spain and Portugal without fear;
So with a mighty army three hundred thousand strong
Through the passes of the Pyrenees into Spain he passed
  along.

But Sir John Moore concentrated his troops in the north,
And into the west corner of Spain he boldly marched forth;
To cut off Napoleon's communications with France
He considered it to be advisable and his only chance.

And when Napoleon heard of Moore's coming, his march he
    did begin,
Declaring that he was the only General that could oppose
    him;
And in the month of December, when the hills were clad
    with snow,
Napoleon's army marched over the Guadiana Hills with
    their hearts full of woe.

And with fifty thousand cavalry, infantry, and artillery,
Napoleon marched on, facing obstacles most dismal to see;
And performed one of the most rapid marches recorded in
    history,
Leaving the command of his army to Generals Soult and
    Ney.

And on the 5th of January Soult made his attack,
But in a very short time the French were driven back;
With the Guards and the 50th Regiment and the 42d
  conjoint,
They were driven from the village of Elnina at the bayonet's
  point.

Oh! it was a most gorgeous and inspiring sight
To see Sir John Moore in the thickest of the fight,
And crying aloud to the 42d with all his might,
"Forward, my lads, and charge them with your bayonets
  left and right."

Then the 42d charged them with might and main,
And the French were repulsed again and again;
And although they poured into the British ranks a withering
  fire,
The British at the charge of the bayonet soon made them
  retire.

Oh! that battlefield was a fearful sight to behold,
'Twas enough to make one's blood run cold
To hear the crack, crack of the musketry and the cannon's
  roar,
Whilst the dead and the dying lay weltering in their gore.

But O Heaven! it was a heartrending sight,
When Sir John Moore was shot dead in the thickest of the
  fight;
And as the soldiers bore him from the field they looked
  woebegone,
And the hero's last words were "Let me see how the battle
  goes on."

Then he breathed his last with a gurgling sound,
And for the loss of the great hero the soldiers' sorrow was
  profound,
Because he was always kind and served them well,
And as they thought of him tears down their cheeks trickling
  fell.

Oh! it was a weird and pathetic sight
As they buried him in the Citadel of Corunna at the dead of
  night,
While his staff and the men shed many tears
For the noble hero who had commanded them for many
  years.

Success to the British Army wherever they go,
For seldom they have failed to conquer the foe;
Long may the Highlanders be able to make the foe reel,
By giving them an inch or two of cold steel.

A TALE OF CHRISTMAS EVE

'Twas Christmastide in Germany,
And in the year of 1850,
And in the city of Berlin, which is most beautiful to the eye;
A poor boy was heard calling out to the passers-by.

"Who'll buy my pretty figures," loudly he did cry,
Plaster of Paris figures, but no one inclined to buy;
His clothes were thin and he was nearly frozen with cold,
And wholly starving with hunger, a pitiful sight to behold.

And the twilight was giving place to the shadows of
approaching night,
And those who possessed a home were seeking its warmth
and light;
And the market square was dark and he began to moan,
When he thought of his hungry brother and sisters at home.

Alas! the poor boy was afraid to go home,
Oh, Heaven! hard was his lot, for money he'd none;
And the tears coursed down his cheeks while loudly he did
cry,
"Buy my plaster of Paris figures, oh! please come buy."

It was now quite dark while he stood there,
And the passers-by did at the poor boy stare,
As he stood shivering with cold in the market square;
And with the falling snow he was almost frozen to the bone.
And what would it avail him standing there alone,
Therefore he must make up his mind to return home.

Then he tried to hoist the board and figures on to his head,
And for fear of letting the board fall he was in great dread;
Then he struggled manfully forward without delay,
But alas! he fell on the pavement, oh! horror and dismay.

And his beautiful figures were broken and scattered around
him,
And at the sight thereof his eyes grew dim;
And when he regained his feet he stood speechless like one
bowed down,
Then the poor boy did fret and frown.

Then the almost despairing boy cried aloud,
And related his distress to the increasing crowd;
Oh! What a pitiful sight on a Christmas eve,
But the dense crowd didn't the poor boy relieve,

Until a poor wood-cutter chanced to come along,
And he asked of the crowd what was wrong;
And twenty ready tongues tells him the sad tale,
And when he heard it the poor boy's fate he did bewail.

And he cried, "Here! Something must be done and quickly
    too,
Do you hear! Every blessed soul of you;
Come, each one give a few pence to the poor boy,
And it will help to fill his heart with joy."

Then the wood-cutter gave a golden coin away,
So the crowd subscribed largely without delay;
Which made the poor boy's heart feel gay,
Then the wood-cutter thanked the crowd and went away.

So the poor boy did a large subscription receive,
And his brother, mother, and sisters had a happy Christmas
    eve;
And he thanked the crowd and God that to him the money
    sent,
And bade the crowd good-night, then went home content.

THE BATTLE OF GUJRAT

'Twas in the year of 1849, and on the 20th of February,
Lord Gough met and attacked Shere Sing right manfully.
The Sikh Army numbered 40,000 in strength,
And showing a front about two miles length.

It was a glorious morning, the sun was shining in a cloudless
    sky;
And the larks were singing merrily in the heavens high;
And 'twas about nine o'clock in the morning the battle was
    begun,
But at the end of three hours the Sikhs were forced torun.

Lord Gough's force was a mixture of European and native
    infantry,
And well supported with artillery and cavalry;
But the British Army in numbers weren't so strong,
Yet, fearlessly and steadily, they marched along.

Shere Sing, the King, had taken up a position near the town,
And as he gazed upon the British Army he did frown;
But Lord Gough ordered the troops to commence the battle,
With sixty big guns that loudly did rattle.

The Sikhs were posted on courses of deep water,
But the British in a short time soon did them scatter.
Whilst the British cannonading loudly bums,
And in the distance were heard the enemy's drums.

Then the Sikhs began to fight with their artillery,
But their firing didn't work very effectively;
Then the British lines advanced on them right steadily,
Which was a most inspiring sight to see.

Then the order was given to move forward to attack,
And again—and again—through fear the enemy drew back.
Then Penny's brigade, with a ringing cheer, advanced
    briskly,
And charged with their bayonets very heroically.

Then the Sikhs caught the bayonets with their left hand,
And rushed in with their swords, the scene was heroic and
　　grand.
Whilst they slashed and cut with great dexterity,
But the British charge was irresistible, they had to flee.

And with 150 men they cleared the village of every living
　　thing,
And with British cheers the village did ring;
And the villagers in amazement and terror fled,
Because the streets and their houses were strewn with their
　　dead.

The chief attack was made on the enemy's right
By Colin Campbell's brigade—a most magnificent sight.
Though they were exposed to a very galling fire,
But at last the Sikhs were forced to retire.

And in their flight everything was left behind,
And the poor Sikhs were of all comfort bereft,
Because their swords, cannon, drums, and waggons were left
　　behind,
Therefore little pleasure could they find.

Then Shere Sing fled in great dismay,
But Lord Gough pursued him without delay,
And captured him a few miles away;
And now the Sikhs are our best soldiers of the present day,
Because India is annexed to the British Dominions, and they
　　must obey.

BILL BOWLS THE SAILOR

Bill Bowels was an amiable gentle youth,
And concerning him I'll relate the truth;
His Mother wanted to make him a Tailor,
But Bill's Father said he was cut out for a Sailor.

Dancing bareheaded under heavy rain was his delight,
And wading in ponds and rivers by day and night;
And he was as full of mischief as an Egg is full of meat,
And tumbling and swimming in deep pools to him was a
    treat.

His Father was a Mill Wright, and lived near a small lake,
And many a swim in that lake, Bill used to take;
And many a good lesson his good dad gave to him,
To keep always in shoal water till he could swim.

One day he got hold of a very big plank,
And with it he resolved to play some funny prank,
So he launched the plank into the lake,
Crying now I'll have some rare fun and no mistake.

And on the plank he went with a piece broken paling for an
    oar,
But suddenly a squall came down on the lake which made
    him roar,
And threw him on his beam ends into the water,
And the clothes he had on him were drenched every tatter.

'Twas lucky for Bill his Father heard his cries,
And to save poor Bill he instantly flies,
And he leaped into the lake and dragged Bill ashore,
While Bill for help did lustily roar.

Then after that he joined a ship bound for China,
With a pair of light breeches and his heart full of glee,
But his heart soon became less buoyant
When he discovered his Captain was a great tyrant.

One evening as Bill stood talking to the steersman,
And the weather at the time was very calm;
Tom Riggles said, Bill we're going to have dirty weather,
But with the help of God, we'll weather it together.

That night the Captain stood holding to on the shrouds,
While scudding across the sky were thick angry clouds
And the ship was running unsteady before the wind,
And the Captain was drunk must be borne in mind.

Then a cry is heard which might have chilled the stoutest
    heart,
Which caused every man on board with fear to start;
Oh! heavens, rocks ahead, shouted the mate, above the gale,
While every face on board turned ghastly pale.

Then, port! port! hard-a-port! shouted the men
All over the ship, from bow to stern,
And the order was repeated by the mate
Who sprang to the wheel, fearlessly resigned to his fate.

At last a heavy wave struck the ship with a terrible dash,
Which made every plank quiver and give way with a crash,
While wave on the back of wave struck her with fearful
    shocks,
Until at last she was lifted up and cast on the rugged rocks.

Oh! heaven, it must have been an awful sight,
To witness in the dusky moon-light;
Men clinging to the rigging with all their might,
And others trying to put the ship all right.

Then the wind it blew a terrific blast,
Which tore the rigging away and the missen-mast;
And the big waves lashed her furiously,
And the Captain was swept with the wreck into the sea.

Then every man struggled manfully to gain the shore,
While the storm fiend did loudly laugh and roar,
But alas! they all perished but Tom Riggles and Bill Bowls,
And they were cast on a rocky islet where on the tempest
    howls

And they lived on shell fish while they were there,
Until one day they began to despair,
But thank God they espied a vessel near at hand,
And they were taken on board and landed safe in fair
    England.

THE BATTLE OF THE ALMA.   FOUGHT IN 1854

'Twas on the heights of Alma the battle began,
But the Russians turned and fled every man;
Because Sir Colin Campbell's Highland Brigade put them to
    flight,
At the charge of the bayonet, which soon ended the fight.

Sir Colin Campbell he did loudly cry,
Let the Highlanders go forward, they will win or die,
We'll hae nane but Hieland bonnets here,
So forward, my lads, and give one ringing cheer.

Then boldly and quickly they crossed the river,
But not one amongst them with fear did shiver,
And ascended the height, forming quietly on the crest,
While each man seemed anxious to do his best.

The battle was fought by twenty against one,
But the gallant British troops resolved to die to a man,
While the shot was mowing them down and making ugly
    gaps,
And shells shrieking and whistling and making fearful
    cracks.

On the heights of Alma it was a critical time,
And to see the Highland Brigade it was really sublime,
To hear the officers shouting to their men,
On lads, I'll show you the way to fight them.

Close up! Close up! Stand firm, my boys,
Now be steady, men, steady and think of our joys;
If we only conquer the Russians this day,
Our fame will be handed down to posterity for ever and aye.

Still forward! Forward! my lads was the cry,
And from the redoubt make them fly;
And at length the Russians had to give way,
And fled from the redoubt in wild dismay.

Still the fate of the battle hung in the balance,
But Sir Colin knew he had still a chance,
But one weak officer in fear loudly shouted,
Let the Guards fall back, or they'll be totally routed.

Then Sir Colin Campbell did make reply,
'Tis better, Sir, that every man of the Guards should die,
And to be found dead on this bloody field,
Than to have it said they fled and were forced to yield.

Then the Coldstreams on the Highlanders' right
Now advanced to engage the enemy in the fight,
But then they halted, unable to go forward,
Because the Russians did their progress retard.

But now came the turning point of the battle,
While the Russian guns loudly did rattle;
Then Sir Colin turned to the plumed Highland array,
And in stirring tones to them did say—

Be steady, keep silence, my lads, don't be afraid,
And make me proud of my Highland Brigade;
Then followed the command, sharp and clear,
While the war notes of the 42d bagpipes smote the ear.

The soldiers, though young, were cool and steady,
And to face the enemy they were ever ready,
And still as the bare-kneed line unwavering came on
It caused the Russians to shake and look woebegone.

And now as the din of the fight grew greater,
Fear filled the hearts of the Russian giants in stature,
Because the kilted heroes they fought so well
That they thought they had come from the regions of hell.

Oh! it was a most beautiful and magnificent display
To see the Highland Brigade in their tartan array,
And their tall bending plumes in a long line,
The scene was inspiring and really sublime.

Then, terror-stricken by this terrible advancing line,
The Russians broke down and began to whine,
And they turned round and fled with a moaning cry,
Because they were undone and had to fly.

Then the crisis was past and the victory won,
Which caused Sir Colin Campbell to cry, Well done,
And, raising his hand, gave the signal to cheer,
Which was responded to by hurrahs, loud and clear.

BEAUTIFUL ROTHESAY

Beautiful Rothesay, your scenery is most grand,
You cannot be surpassed in fair Scotland.
Tis healthy for holiday makers, to go there,
For the benefit of their health, by inhaling the pure air

And to hear the innocent birds, on a fine Summer day,
Carolling their sweet songs, so lively and gay,
Therefore, holiday makers, be advised by me,
And visit beautiful Rothesay, by the side of the Sea.

Then Sweet Jessie, let us go,
To Scotlands garden of Eden O!
And spend the lovely Summer day,
In the beautiful village of Rothesay.

There you can see the ships, passing to and fro,
Which will drive away dull care, and woe,
And, the heavens breath smells wooingly there,
Therefore, lets away dear Jessie, to inhale the balmy air.

The mansions, there, are most beautiful to be seen,
Likewise the trees, and shrubberies, green.
Therefore, we will feel happy and gay,
Walking hand in hand, together the live long day.

Along the beautiful walks with our hearts fu' cheerie,
My dear love! until we grow weary.
Then, return home at night, with our spirits light and gay,
After viewing the beautiful scenery of Rothesay.

THE BATTLE OF INKERMANN

'Twas in the year of 1854, and on the 5th of November,
Which Britain will no doubt long remember,
When the Russians plotted to drive the British army into
    the sea,
But at the bayonet charge the British soon made them flee.

With fourteen hundred British, fifteen thousand Russians
    were driven back,
At half-past seven o'clock in the morning they made the
    attack,
But the Grenadiers and Scottish Fusilier Guards, seven
    hundred strong,
Moved rapidly and fearlessly all along.

And their rifles were levelled ready for a volley,
But the damp had silenced their fire which made the men
feel melancholy,
But the Russians were hurled down the ravine in a
disordered mass
At the charge of the bayonet—an inspiring sight!—nothing
could it surpass.

General Cathcart thought he could strike a blow at an
unbroken Russian line;
Oh! the scene was really very sublime,
Because hand to hand they fought with a free will,
And with one magnificent charge they hurled the Russians
down the hill.

But while General Cathcart without any dread
Was collecting his scattered forces, he fell dead,
Pierced to the heart with a Russian ball,
And his men lamented sorely his downfall.

While the Duke of Cambridge with the colours of two
Regiments of Guards
Presses forward, and no obstacle his courage retards,
And with him about one hundred men,
And to keep up their courage he was singing a hymn to them.

Then hand to hand they fought the Russians heroically,
Which was a most inspiring sight to see;
Captain Burnaby with thirteen Guardsmen fighting
manfully,
And they drove the Russians down the hillside right
speedily.

The French and Zouaves aided the British in the fight,
And they shot down and killed the Russians left and right,
And the Chasseurs also joined in the fight,
And the Russians fell back in great afright.

Then the Russians tried again and again
To drive the British from the slopes of Inkermann, but all in
    vain,
For the French and British beat them back without dismay,
Until at last the Russians had to give way.

And the French and British fought side by side
Until the Russians no longer the bayonet charge could abide,
And the Russians were literally scorched by the musketry
    fire,
And in a short time the Russians were forced to retire.

Then the British and French pursued them into the depths
    of the ravine,
Oh! it was a grand sight—the scene was really sublime—
And at half-past one o'clock the Russians were defeated,
And from the field of Inkermann they sullenly retreated.

Then the Battle of Inkermann was won,
And from the field the Russians were forced to run,
But the loss of the British was terrible to behold;
The dead lay in heaps stiff and cold,
While thousands of Russians were dying with no one to aid
    them,
Alas! pitiful to relate, thousands of innocent men.

LITTLE PIERRE'S SONG

In a humble room in London sat a pretty little boy,
By the bedside of his sick mother her only joy,
Who was called Little Pierre, and who's father was dead;
There he sat poor boy, hungry and crying for bread.

There he sat humming a little song, which was his own,
But to the world it was entirely unknown,
And as he sang the song he felt heartsick,
But he resolved to get Madame Malibran to sing his song in
    public

Then he paused for a moment and clasped his hands,
And running to the looking-glass before it he stands,
Then he smoothed his yellow curls without delay,
And from a tin box takes a scroll of paper worn and grey.

Then he gave one fond eager glance at his mother,
Trying hard brave boy his grief to smother,
As he gazed on the bed where she lay,
But he resolved to see Madame Malibran without delay.

Then he kissed his mother while she slept,
And stealthly from the house he crept,
And direct to Madame Malibran's house he goes,
Resolved to see her no matter who did him oppose.

And when he reached the door he knocked like a brave
    gallant
And the door was answered by her lady servant,
Then he told the servant Madame Malibran he wished to see
And the servant said, oh yes, I'll tell her immediately.

Then away the servant goes feeling quite confident,
And told her a little boy wished to see her just one moment
Oh! well, said Madame Malibran, with a smile,
Fetch in the little boy he will divert me a while.

So Little Pierre was brought in with his hat under his arm
And in his hand a scroll of paper, thinking it no harm,
Then walked straight up to Madame Malibran without dread
And said, dear lady my mother is sick and in want of bread.

And I have called to see if you would sing my little song,
At some of your grand concerts, Ah! say before long,
Or perhaps you could sell it to a publisher for a small sum,
Then I could buy food for my mother and with it would run.

Then Madame Malibran rose from her seat most costly and
     grand
And took the scroll of paper from Pierre's hand
And hummed his little song, to a plaintive air,
Then said, your song is soul stirring I do declare.

Dear child did you compose the words she asked Pierre,
Oh yes my dear lady just as you see,
Well my dear boy I will sing your song to-night,
And you shall have a seat near me on the right.

Then Pierre, said, Oh! lady I cannot leave my mother,
But my dear boy, as for her you need not bother,
So dear child don't be the least cast down,
And in the meantime here is a crown.

And for your mother you can buy food and medicine,
So run away and be at the concert to-night in time
Then away he ran and bought many little necessary things
And while doing so his little song he hums and sings.

Then home to his poor sick mother he quickly ran,
And told her of his success with Madame Malibran,
Then his mother cried, Oh! Pierre, you are a very good boy,
And to hear of your success my heart is full of joy.

Dear mother, I am going to the concert hall to-night,
To hear Madame Malibran, which will my heart delight,
Oh! well said his mother, God speed you my little man,
I hope you will be delighted to hear Madame Malibran.

So to the concert hall he goes, and found a seat there,
And the lights and flashing of diamonds made him stare,
And caused a joyous smile to play upon his face,
For never had he been in so grand a place.

There the brave boy sat and Madame Malibran came at last
And with his eyes rivetted on her he stared aghast,
And to hear her sing, Oh! how he did long,
And he wondered if the lady would really sing his song.

At last the great singer commenced his little song,
And many a heart was moved and the plaudits loud and
    long
And as she sang it Pierre clapped his hands for joy.
That he felt as it were free from the world's annoy.

When the concert was over his heart felt as light as the air
And as for money now he didn't seem to care,
Since the great singer in Europe had sung his little song,
But he hoped that dame fortune would smile on him ere
    long

The next day he was frightened by a visit from Madame
    Malibran
And turning to his mother, she said your little boy Madame
Will make a fortune for himself and you before long,
Because I've been offered a large sum for his little song.

And Madame thank God you have such a gifted son,
But dear Madame heavens will must be done,
Then Pierre knelt and prayed that God would the lady bless
For helping them in the time of their distress.

And the memory of Pierre's prayer made the singer do more
    good
By visiting the poor and giving them clothing and food
And Pierre lightened her last moments ere her soul fled away
And he came to be one of the most talented composers of the
    day.

THE CAPTURE OF LUCKNOW

'Twas near the Begum Kothie the battle began,
Where innocent blood as plentiful as water ran;
The Begum Kothie was a place of honour given to the 93rd,
Which heroically to a man they soon did begird.

53

And the 4th Punjaub Rifles were their companions in glory,
And are worthy of their names enrolled in story,
Because they performed prodigious wonders in the fight,
By killing and scattering the Sepoys left and right.

The 93rd Highlanders bivouacked in a garden surrounded
   by mud walls,
Determined to capture the Begum Kothie no matter what
   befalls—,
A place strongly fortified and of enormous strength,
And protected by strong earthworks of very great length.

And added to these obstacles was the most formidable of
   all—
A broad deep ditch that ran along the wall,
Which the storming party not even guessed at before;
But this barrier the British soon did climb o'er.

But early the next morning two batteries of Artillery were
   pounding away,
And the fight went on for the whole day;
And the defenders of the building kept up rattling musketry
   fire,
And when night fell the British had to retire.

Next day the contest was renewed with better success,
And the 93rd in all their beauty forward did press,
And moved on toward the position without firing a shot,
And under cover of some ruined buildings they instantly got.

And here for a few minutes they kept themselves under
   cover,
While each man felt more anxious than another
To attack the merciless rebels while it was day,
Because their blood was up and eager for the fray.

Still the enemy kept up a blazing fire at them pell-mell,
But they fired too high and not a man of them fell;
And the bullets whistled around them again and again,
Still on went the unwavering Highlanders with might and
   main.

But when they reached the ditch they were taken by
   surprise,
By the unexpected obstacle right before their eyes;
But Captain Middleton leapt into the ditch and showed
   them the way,
And immediately the whole of the men were after him
   without delay.

Leith Hay himself was among the first across,
And gained a footing on the other side without any personal
   loss;
And he assisted in helping the rest out of the ditch,
While the din of war was at the highest pitch.

'Twas then the struggle commenced in terrible earnest:
While every man was resolved to do his best;
And the enemy barricaded every entrance so as a single man
   could only pass,
Determined to make a strong resistance, and the British to
   harass.

But barrier after barrier soon was passed;
And the brave men no doubt felt a little harassed,
But they fought desperately and overturned their foes at
    every point,
And put the rebels to flight by shot and bayonet conjoint.

The Sheiks and the Horse Guards behaved right well—
Because beneath their swords, by the score, the Sepoys fell;
And their beautiful war steeds did loudly neigh and roar,
While beneath their hoofs they trampled them all o'er.

And as for John McLeod—the pipe-major of the 93rd,
He kept sounding his bagpipes and couldn't be stirred—
Because he remembered his duty in the turmoil,
And in the battlefield he was never known to recoil.

And as for Major General McBain—he was the hero in the
    fight;
He fought heroically—like a lion—with all his might;
And again and again he was met by desperate odds,
But he scattered them around him and made them kiss the
    sods.

And he killed eleven of the enemy with sword in hand,
Which secured for him the proudest of all honours in the
    land,
Namely, that coveted honour called the Victoria Cross,
Of which many a deserving hero has known the loss.

And as for brave Hodson—he was a warrior born,
And military uniform did his body adorn;
And his voice could be heard in the battle afar,
Crying—"Come on my boys there is nothing like war!"

But, in a moment, a volley was discharged at him,
And he fell mortally wounded, while the Sepoys did grin;
Then the Highlanders closed with their foes and made them
    retreat,
And left them not till every rebel lay dead at their feet.

Then Sir Colin Campbell to his men did say,—
"Men, I feel proud that we have captured Lucknow this
    day;
Therefore strike up the bagpipes and give one hearty cheer,
And enjoy yourselves, my heroes, while ye are here."

THE BURNS STATUE
(A fragment)

This Statue, I must confess, is magnificent to see,
And I hope will long be appreciated by the people of Dundee;
It has been beautifully made by Sir John Steell,
And I hope the pangs of hunger he will never feel.

This Statue is most elegant in its design,
And I hope will defy all weathers for a very long time;
And I hope strangers from afar with admiration will stare
On this beautiful statue of thee, Immortal Bard of Ayr.

Fellow-citizens, this Statue seems most beautiful to the eye,
Which would cause Kings and Queens for such a one to sigh,
And make them feel envious while passing by
In fear of not getting such a beautiful Statue after they die.

THE HERO OF KALAPORE : AN INCIDENT
OF THE INDIAN MUTINY

The 27th Regiment has mutinied at Kalapore:

That was the substance of a telegram, which caused a great uproar

At Sattara, on the evening of the 8th of July,

And when the British officers heard it, they heaved a bitter sigh.

'Twas in the year of 1857,

Which will long be remembered : Oh! Heaven!

That the Sepoys revolted, and killed their British officers and their wives;

Besides, they killed their innocent children, not sparing one of their lives.

There was one man there who was void of fear,

He was the brave Lieutenant William Alexander Kerr;

And to face the rebels boldly it was his intent,

And he assured his brother officers his men were true to the Government.

And now that the danger was so near at hand,

He was ready to put his men to the test, and them command;

And march to the rescue of his countrymen at Kalapore,

And try to quell the mutiny and barbarous uproar.

And in half an hour he was ready to start,

With fifty brave horsemen, fearless and smart;

And undaunted Kerr and his horsemen rode on without dismay,

And in the middle of the rainy season, which was no child's play.

And after a toilsome march they reached Kalapore,
To find their countrymen pressed very hard and sore;
The mutineers had attacked and defeated the Kalapore
  Light Infantry,
Therefore their fellow countrymen were in dire extremity.

Then the Sepoys established themselves in a small square
  fort;
It was a place of strength, and there they did resort;
And Kerr had no guns to batter down the gate,
But nevertheless he felt undaunted, and resigned to his
  fate.

And darkness was coming on and no time was to be lost,
And he must attack the rebels whatever be the cost;
Therefore he ordered his troopers to prepare to storm the
  fort,
And at the word of command towards it they did resort.

And seventeen troopers advanced to the attack,
And one of his men, Gumpunt Row Deo Kerr, whose
  courage wasn't slack;
So great was his courage he couldn't be kept back,
So he resolved with Lieutenant Kerr to make the attack.

Then with crowbars they dashed at the doors vigorously,
Whilst bullets rained around them, but harmlessly;
So they battered on the doors until one gave way,
Then Lieutenant Kerr and his henchmen entered without
  dismay.

Then Kerr's men rushed in sword in hand,
Oh! what a fearful onslaught, the mutineers couldn't it
    withstand,
And Kerr's men with straw set the place on fire,
And at last the rebels were forced to retire.

And took refuge in another house, and barricaded it fast,
And prepared to defend themselves to the last;
Then Lieutenant Kerr and Row Deo Kerr plied the
    crowbars again,
And heavy blows on the woodwork they did rain.

Then the door gave way and they crawled in,
And they two great heroes side by side did begin
To charge the mutineers with sword in hand, which made
    them grin,
Whilst the clashing of swords and bayonets made a fearful
    din.

Then hand to hand, and foot to foot, a fierce combat
    began,
Whilst the blood of the rebels copiously ran,
And a ball cut the chain of Kerr's helmet in two,
And another struck his sword, but the man he slew.

Then a Sepoy clubbed his musket and hit Kerr on the
    head,
But fortunately the blow didn't kill him dead;
He only staggered, and was about to be bayoneted by a
    mutineer,
But Gumpunt Kerr laid his assailant dead without fear.

Kerr's little party were now reduced to seven,
Yet fearless and undaunted, and with the help of Heaven,
He gathered his small band possessed of courage bold,
Determined to make a last effort to capture the stronghold.

Then he cried, "My men, we will burn them out,
And suffocate them with smoke, without any doubt!"
So bundles of straw and hay were found without delay,
And they set fire to them against the doors without dismay.

Then Kerr patiently waited till the doors were consumed,
And with a gallant charge, the last attack was resumed,
And he dashed sword in hand into the midst of the
    mutineers,
And he and his seven troopers played great havoc with their
    sabres.

So by the skillful war tactics of brave Lieutenant Kerr,
He defeated the Sepoy mutineers and rescued his country-
    men dear;
And but for Lieutenant Kerr the British would have met
    with a great loss,
And for his great service he received the Victoria Cross.

JACK HONEST, OR THE WIDOW AND HER SON

Jack Honest was only eight years of age when his father
    died,
And by the death of his father, Mrs Honest was sorely
    tried;
And Jack was his father's only joy and pride,
And for honesty Jack couldn't be equalled in the
    country-side.

So a short time before Jack's father died,
'Twas loud and bitterly for Jack he cried,
And bade him sit down by his bedside,
And then told him to be honest whatever did betide.

John, he said, looking him earnestly in the face,
Never let your actions your name disgrace,
Remember, my dear boy, and do what's right,
And God will bless you by day and night.

Then Mr Honest bade his son farewell, and breathed his
    last,
While the hot tears from Jack's eyes fell thick and fast;
And the poor child did loudly sob and moan,
When he knew his father had left him and his mother
    alone.

So, as time wore on, Jack grew to be a fine boy,
And was to his mother a help and a joy;
And, one evening, she said, Jack, you are my only prop,
I must tell you, dear, I'm thinking about opening a shop.

Oh! that's a capital thought, mother, cried Jack,
And to take care of the shop I won't be slack;
Then his mother said, Jackey, we will try this plan,
And look to God for his blessing, and do all we can.

So the widow opened the shop and succeeded very well,
But in a few months fresh troubles her befell—
Alas! poor Mrs Honest was of fever taken ill,
But Jack attended his mother with a kindly will.

But, for fear of catching the fever, her customers kept
  away,
And once more there wasn't enough money the rent to
  pay;
And in her difficulties Mrs Honest could form no plan to
  get out,
But God would help her, she had no doubt.

So, one afternoon, Mrs Honest sent Jack away
To a person that owed her some money, and told him not
  to stay,
But when he got there the person had fled,
And to return home without the money he was in
  dread.

So he saw a gentleman in a carriage driving along at a
  rapid rate,
And Jack ran forward to his mansion and opened the
  lodge-gate,
Then the gentleman opened his purse and gave him, as he
  thought, a shilling
For opening the lodge-gate so cleverly and so willing.

Then Jack stooped to lift up the coin, when, lo and
  behold!
He found to his surprise it was a piece of gold!
And Jack cried oh! joyful, this will make up my mother's
  loss,
Then he ran home speedily, knowing his mother wouldn't
  be cross.

And when he got home he told his mother of his ill
   success,
And his adventure with the gentleman, then she felt deep
   distress;
And when Jack showed her the sovereign, the gentleman
   gave him,
She cried, We mustn't keep that money, it would be a sin.

Dear mother, I thought so, there must be some mistake,
But in the morning, to Squire Brooksby, the sovereign
   I'll take;
So, when morning came, he went to Squire Brooksby's
   Hall,
And at the front door for the Squire he loudly did call.

Then the hall door was opened by a footman, dressed in
   rich livery,
And Jack told him he wished Mr Brooksby to see;
Then to deliver Jack's message the footman withdrew,
And when the footman returned he said, Master will see you.

Then Jack was conducted into a rich furnished room,
And to Mr Brooksby he told his errand very soon,
While his honest heart, with fear, didn't quake,
Saying, Mr Brooksby, you gave me a sovereign yesterday
   in a mistake.

Why, surely I have seen you before, said Mr Brooksby;
Yes, Sir, replied Jack Honest, bowing very politely;
Then what is your name, my honest lad ? asked Mr
   Brooksby;
John Honest, sir, replied Jack, right fearlessly.

Then, my brave lad, you are Honest by name, and honest
   by nature,
Which, really, you appear to be in every feature,
But, I am afraid, such boys as you are very few,
But, I dare say, your mother has taught you.

Then Jack laid the sovereign down on the table before
   Mr Brooksby;
But Mr Brooksby said, No! my lad, I freely give it to thee;
Then Jack said, Oh, sir, I'm obliged to you I'm sure,
Because, sir, this money will help my mother, for she is
   poor.

Mrs Brooksby came to see Mrs Honest in a few days,
And for Jack's honesty she was loud in praise;
And she took Jack into her service, and paid him liberally,
And she gave Mrs Honest a house, for life, rent free.

Now, I must leave Jack Honest and his mother in fresh-
   found glory,
Hoping my readers will feel interested in this story,
And try always to imitate the hero—Jack Honest—
And I'm sure they will find it the safest and the best!

THE DOWNFALL OF DELHI

'Twas in the year of 1857 and on the 14th of September
That the Sepoy rebels at Delhi were forced to surrender;
The attack was first to be made by Brigadier Nicholson,
And he was ordered to attack the Cashmere Bastion.

The British were entirely in command
Of Major-General Reid, assisted by Brigadier-Generals
   Wilson and Burnand;
After a long march, fighting through a hostile country,
And the brave heroes took up a position before the city.

Delhi gates were encircled with a fringe of fire,
But the British resolved to die rather than retire;
And the brave fellows rushed towards the gate
Carrying the powder bags that were to seal the Sepoys'
   fate.

Here their progress was checked, for the drawbridge was
   destroyed,
But the British felt very little annoyed,
Because a few planks were across the chasm thrown,
Then a match was applied to the powder bags, and into
   atoms the gate was blown.

Then the rebel artillerymen with terror fled,
For the streets were strewn by the Sepoy dead;
Then the British charged them without fear,
Shouting "On boys, on, for our Queen and Country dear."

Then Lieutenant Home gave orders to advance,
And charge them with your bayonets, it is our only
   chance;
And with a ringing British cheer they charged them
   fearlessly,
And they drove the enemy before them through the
   streets of the city.

Then the young bugler blew a blast loud and clear,
Which was answered by a British ringing cheer;
But General Nicholson was killed, which was a great loss,
And afterwards the bugler was decorated with the Victoria
  Cross.

General Jones formed a junction with Colonel Campbell's
  Regiment,
And to enter by the Cashmere Gate they were bent;
And they advanced through the streets without delay,
And swept all before them through the gate without
  dismay.

The streets were filled with mutineers who fought
  savagely,
Determined to fight to the last and die heroically,
While the alarm drums did beat, and the cannons did roar,
And the dead and the dying lay weltering in their gore.

And the rebels fought for King Timour like tigers in a cage,
He was a very old man, more than ninety years of age;
And their shouts and yells were fearful to hear,
While the shrill sound of the bugle smote on the ear.

The British dash at Delhi will never be forgot,
For the chief instigators of the mutiny were shot;
And their bodies in the Mayor's Court were hung,
And as the people gazed thereon, their hearts with anguish
  were wrung.

And that evening General Wilson drank the health of the
  Queen,
Also his officers hailed her Empress of India, which
  enhanced the scene;
While the assembled thousands shouted "God save the
  Queen!"
Oh! it was a most beautiful scene.

Delhi was a glorious prize, for the city was full of jewels
  and gold,
Besides a hundred pieces of cannon, be it told;
But dearly was the victory gained,
But in the book of fame the British are famed;
Oh, it was a glorious and heroic victory,
And will be handed down to posterity.

THE RIVER OF LEITH

As I stood upon the Dean Bridge and viewed the beautiful
  scenery,
I felt fascinated and my heart was full of glee,
And I exclaimed in an ecstasy of delight,
In all my travels I never saw such a sight.

The scenery is so enchanting to look upon
That all tourists will say, "Dull care, be gone."
'Tis certainly a most lovely spot,
And once seen it can never be forgot.

Then away! away! to the River of Leith,
That springs from the land of heather and heath,
And view the gorgeous scenery on a fine summer day.
I'm sure it will drive dull care away.

The water-fall near the Bridge is most beautiful to be
    seen,
As it falls and shines like crystal in the sunsheen;
And the sound can be heard all day long,
While the innocent trouts sing an aquatic song.

The glen is a cool spot in the summer time.
There the people can be shaded from the sunshine
Under the spreading branches of the big trees,
And there's seats there to rest on if they please.

Then near St. Bernard's Well there's a shady bower,
Where the lovers, if they like, can spend an hour;
And while they rest there at their ease
They can make love to each other if they please.

The water of St. Bernard's Well is very nice,
But to get a drink of it one penny is the price.
I think in justice the price is rather high,
To give a penny for a drink when one feels dry.

The braes of the River Leith is most charming to be seen,
With its beautiful trees and shrubberies green,
And as the tourist gazes on the river in the valley below,
His heart with joy feels all aglow.

There the little trouts do sport and play
During the live-long summer day,
While the bee and butterfly is on the wing,
And with the singing of birds the glen doth ring.

The walk underneath the Dean Bridge is lovely to see.
And as ye view the scenery it will fill your heart with glee.
It is good for the people's health to be walking there
As they gaze on the beauties of Nature and inhale pure
    air.

The Dean Bridge is a very magnificent sight,
Because from the basement it is a great height.
And it seems most attractive to the eye,
And arrests the attention of strangers as they pass by.

The braes of Belgrave Crescent is lovely to see,
With its beautiful walks and green shrubbery.
'Tis health for the people that lives near by there
To walk along the bonny walks and breathe the sweet air.

Therefore all lovers of the picturesque, be advised by me
And the beautiful scenery of the River Leith go and see,
And I am sure you will get a very great treat,
Because the River of Leith scenery cannot be beat.

THE ASHANTEE WAR.   THE FALL OF COOMASSIE

'Twas in the year of 1874, and on New Year's Day,
The British Army landed at Elmina without dismay,
And numbering in all, 1400 bayonets strong,
And all along the Cape Coast they fearlessly marched
    along,
Under the command of Sir Garnet Wolseley, a hero bold,
And an honour to his King and country, be it told.

And between them and Coomassie, lay a wilderness of
  jungle,
But they marched on boldly without making a stumble,
And under a tropical sun, upwards of an hundred miles,
While their bayonets shone bright as they marched on in
  files.

Coomassie had to be reached and King Coffee's power
  destroyed,
And, before that was done the British were greatly
  annoyed,
Lieutenant Lord Gifford, with his men gained the Crest of
  the Adenisi Hills,
And when they gained the top, with joy their hearts fills.

Sir John McLeod was appointed General of the Black
  Brigade,
And a great slaughter of the enemy they made,
And took possession of an Ashantee village,
And fought like lions in a fearful rage.

While the British troops most firmly stood,
And advanced against a savage horde concealed in a wood,
Yet the men never flinched, but entered the wood fearlessly,
And all at once the silence was broken by a roar of musketry.

And now the fight began in real earnest,
And the Black Watch men resolved to do their best,
While the enemy were ambushed in the midst of the wood,
Yet the Highlanders their ground firmly stood.

And the roar of the musketry spread through the jungle,
Still the men crept on without making a stumble,
And many of the Black Watch fell wounded and dead,
And Major Macpherson was wounded, but he rallied his
    men without dread.

The battle raged for five hours, but the Highlanders were
    gaining ground,
Until the bagpipes struck up their wild clarion sound,
Then the dusky warriors fled in amazement profound,
Because their comrades were falling on every side around.

Sir Archibald Alison led on the Highland Brigade,
And great havoc amongst the enemy they made,
And village after village they captured and destroyed,
Until King Coffee lost heart and felt greatly annoyed.

Sir John McLeod took the command of his own regiment,
And with a swinging pace into the jaws of death they
    went,
Fearlessly firing by companies in rotation,
And dashed into a double Zone of Fire without hesitation.

And in that manner the Black Watch pressed onward,
And the enemy were powerless their progress to retard,
Because their glittering bayonets were brought into play,
And panic stricken the savage warriors fled in great dismay.

Then Sir Garnet Wolseley with his men entered Coomassie
    at night,
Supported by half the rifles and Highlanders—a most
    beautiful sight,
And King Coffee and his army had fled,
And thousands of his men on the field were left dead.

And King Coffee, he was crushed at last,
And the poor King felt very downcast,
And his sorrow was really profound,
When he heard that Coomassie was burned to the ground.

Then the British embarked for England without delay,
And with joy their hearts felt gay,
And by the end of March they reached England,
And the reception they received was very grand.

THE BEAUTIFUL CITY OF PERTH

Beautiful and ancient city of Perth,
One of the grandest upon the earth,
With your stately mansions and streets so clean,
And situated betwixt two Inches green,
Which are most magnificent to be seen.

The North Inch is beautiful to behold,
Where the daisies and butter-cups their petals unfold,
In the warm summer time of the year,
While the clear silvery Tay rolls by quite near,
And such a scene will your spirits cheer.

The South Inch is lovely, be it said,
And a splendid spot for military parade,
While along the highway there are some big trees,
Where the soldiers can rest or stand at ease,
Whichever way their commanders please.

The surrounding woodland scenery is very grand,
It cannot be surpassed in fair Scotland,
Especially the elegant Palace of Scone, in history renowned,
Where some of Scotland's kings were crowned.

And the Fair Maid of Perth's house is worthy to be seen,
Which is well worth visiting by Duke, Lord, or Queen;
The Fair Maid of Perth caused the battle on the North Inch
'Twixt the Clans Chattan and Kay, and neither of them did
    flinch,
Until they were cut up inch by inch.

The scenery is lovely in the month of June,
When trees and flowers are in full bloom,
Especially near by the Palace of Scone,
Where the blackbird is heard whistling all day
While near by rolls on the clear silvery Tay.

Of all the cities in Scotland, beautiful Perth for me,
For it is the most elegant city that ever I did see,
With its beautiful woodland scenery along the river Tay,
Which would make the tourist's heart feel gay,
While fishing for trout on a fine summer day.

There, the angler, if he likes to resort
For a few day's fishing, can have excellent sport,
And while he is fishing during the day,
He will feel delighted with the scenery along the river Tay.
And the fish he catches will drive dull care away,
And his toil will be rewarded for the fatigues of the day.

Beautiful city of Perth, magnificent to be seen,
With your grand statues and Inches green,
And your lovely maidens fair and gay,
Which, in conclusion, I will venture to say,
You cannot be surpassed at the present day.

GENERAL ROBERTS IN AFGHANISTAN

'Twas in the year of 1878, and the winter had set in,
Lord Roberts and the British Army their march did begin,
On their way to Afghanistan to a place called Cabul;
And the weather was bitter cold and the rivers swollen and
   full.

And the enemy were posted high up amongst the hills,
And when they saw the British, with fear their blood thrills;
The savages were camped on the hillsides in war array,
And occupying a strong position which before the British
   lay.

And viewed from the front their position was impregnable,
But Lord Roberts was a general of great skill;
Therefore to surprise the enemy he thought it was right,
To march upon the enemy in the dead of night.

Then the men were mustered without delay,
And each man of them was eager for the fray;
And in the silent darkness they felt no dismay,
And to attack the enemy they marched boldly away.

And on they marched bravely without fear or doubt,
And about daybreak the challenge of an Afghan sentinel
   rang out,
And echoed from rock to rock on the frosty biting air;
But the challenge didn't the British scare.

Then the Highlanders attacked them left and right,
And oh! it was a gorgeous and an inspiring sight;
For a fierce hand to hand struggle raged for a time,
While the pibrochs skirled aloud, oh! the scene was
   sublime.

Then the Ghoorkas did the Afghans fiercely attack,
And at every point and turning they were driven back;
And a fierce hand to hand struggle raged for a time,
While in the morning sunshine the British bayonets did
    shine.

And around the ridge or knoll the battle raged for three
    hours,
And British bullets fell amongst them in showers;
For Captain Kelso brought us his mountain battery,
And sent his shells right into the camp of the enemy,
Then the left of the Afghans was turned, and began to flee.

Meanwhile, on the enemy's strong position Lord Roberts
    launched an attack,
And from their position they could hardly be driven back
Because the Afghans were hid amongst the woods and hills,
Still with undaunted courage, the British blood thrills.

And the Afghans pressed the British hotly, but they didn't
    give way,
For the 8th Ghoorkas and the 72nd kept them at bay;
And the mountain guns shells upon them did fire,
Then the 8th Punjaub, bounding up the heights, made
    them retire.

Then Major White seized a rifle from one of his men and
    did retire,
And levelled the piece fearlessly and did fire;
And with a steady and well-timed shot
He shot the Afghan leader dead on the spot.

Then the British with a wild cheer dashed at them,
And on each side around they did them hem;
And at the bayonet charge they drove them down the hill,
And in hundreds they did them kill.

Then in a confused mass they fled down the opposite side
   of the hill
In hundreds, driven by sheer force sore against their will;
And helter-skelter they did run,
For all their positions were carried and the victory won.

Then on the 8th of August again Lord Roberts' march
   began
For to fight the rebel Ayoob Khan;
And with an army about seven thousand strong
On his way to Candahar he fearlessly marched along.

And the battle that followed at Candahar was a complete
   victory,
And Lord Roberts' march to Candahar stands unrivalled
   in history;
And let's thank God that sent Lord Roberts to conquer
   Ayoob Khan,
For from that time there's been no more war in
   Afghanistan.

Success to Lord Roberts; he's a very brave man,
For he conquered the Afghans in Afghanistan,
With an army about seven thousand strong,
He spread death and desolation all along.

FAREWELL ADDRESS AT THE ARGYLE HALL, TUESDAY, JUNE 22, 1880

Fellow Citizens of Dundee.
I now must bid farewell to ye.
For I am going to London far away.
But when I will return again I cannot say.

Farewell! Farewell! to the bonnie banks o' the Silvery Tay.
Also the beautiful Hill o' Balgay.
And the ill fated Bridge o' the Silvery Tay.
Which I will remember when I am far away.

Farewell! to my friends and patrons all.
That rallied around me in the Music Hall.
And those that has rallied around me to night,
I shall not forget when out of sight.

And if I ever return to Dundee again,
I hope it will be with the laurels of fame.
Plac'd on my brow by dame fortune that fickle Jade.
And to Court her favour I am not afraid.

Farewell! to every one in the Argyle Hall.
That has Come to hear McGonagall.
Recite, and sing, his Songs to night.
Which I hope will long be remember'd when I'm out of
    sight.

Adieu to all my enemies that want to mock me when
    passing by.
But I excuse them for their ignorance and leave them to
    the most high.
And, once again, my friends, and enemies. I bid ye all
    good bye.
And when I am gone ye will for me heave a sigh :—

78

I return my thanks to my Chairman and my Committee,
For the Kindness they have always shown to me.
I hope the Lord! will protect them when I am far away.
And prosper them in all their undertakings by night and
    by day.

THE LAST BERKSHIRE ELEVEN: THE HEROES OF MAIWAND

'Twas at the disastrous battle of Maiwand, in Afghanistan,
Where the Berkshires were massacred to the last man;
On the morning of July the 27th, in the year eighteen
    eighty,
Which I'm sorry to relate was a pitiful sight to see.

Ayoub Khan's army amounted to twelve thousand in all,
And honestly speaking it wasn't very small,
And by such a great force the Berkshires were killed to the
    last man,
By a murderous rebel horde under the command of Ayoub
    Khan.

The British force amounted to about 2000 strong in all,
But although their numbers were but few it didn't them
    appal;
They were commanded by General Burrows, a man of
    courage bold,
But, alas! the British army was defeated be it told.

The 66th Berkshire Regiment stood as firm as a wall,
Determined to conquer or die whatever would befall,
But in the face of overwhelming odds, and covered to the
last,
The broken and disordered Sepoys were flying fast

Before the victorious Afghan soldiers, whose cheers on the
air arose,
But the gallant band poured in deadly volleys on their foes;
And, outnumbered and surrounded, they fell in sections like
ripe grain;
Still the heroes held their ground, charging with might and
main.

The British force, alas! were shut up like sheep in a pen,
Owing to the bad position General Burrows had chosen for
his men;
But Colonel Galbraith with the Berkshires held the enemy
at bay,
And had the Sepoys been rallied the Afghans would not
have won the day.

But on the Berkshires fell the brunt of the battle,
For by the Afghan artillery they fell like slaughtered
cattle;
Yet the wild horsemen were met with ringing volleys of
musketry,
Which emptied many a saddle; still the Afghans fought
right manfully.

And on came the white cloud like a whirlwind;
But the gallant Berkshires, alas! no help could find,
While their blood flowed like water on every side around,
And they fell in scores, but the men rallied and held their
ground

The brave Berkshires under Colonel Galbraith stood firm in
    the centre there,
Whilst the shouts of the wild Ghazis rent the air;
But still the Berkshires held them at bay,
At the charge of the bayonet, without dismay.

Then the Ghazis, with increased numbers, made another
    desperate charge
On that red line of British bayonets, which wasn't very
    large;
And the wild horsemen were met again with ringing volleys
    of musketry,
Which was most inspiring and frightful to see.

Then Ayoub concentrated his whole attack on the Berkshire
    Regiment,
Which made them no doubt feel rather discontent,
And Jacob's Rifles and the Grenadiers were a confused and
    struggling mass,
Oh heaven! such a confused scene, nothing could it surpass.

But the Berkshires stood firm, replying to the fire of the
    musketry,
While they were surrounded on all sides by masses of
    cavalry;
Still that gallant band resolved to fight for their Queen and
    country,
Their motto being death before dishonour, rather than flee.

At last the gallant British soldiers made a grand stand,
While most of the officers were killed fighting hand to hand,
And at length the Sepoys fled from the enclosure, panic-
    stricken and irate,
Alas! leaving behind their European comrades to their fate.

The Berkshires were now reduced to little more than one
    hundred men,
Who were huddled together like sheep in a pen;
But they broke loose from the enclosure, and back to back,
Poured volley after volley in the midst of the enemy, who
    wern't slack.

And one by one they fell, still the men fought without
    dismay,
And the regimental pet dog stuck to the heroes throughout
    the day;
And their cartridge pouches were empty, and of shot they
    were bereft,
And eleven men, most of them wounded, were all that were
    left.

And they broke from the enclosure, and followed by the
    little dog,
And with excitement it was barking savagely, and leaping
    like a frog;
And from the field the last eleven refused to retire,
And with fixed bayonets they charged on the enemy in that
    sea of fire.

Oh, heaven! it was a fearful scene the horrors of that
    day,
When I think of so many innocent lives that were taken
    away;
Alas! the British force were massacred in cold blood,
And their blood ran like a little rivulet in full flood.

And the Ghazis were afraid to encounter that gallant little
    band
At the charge of the bayonet : Oh! the scene was most
    grand;
And the noble and heroic eleven fought on without dismay,
Until the last man in the arms of death stiff and stark lay.

THE SUNDERLAND CALAMITY

'Twas in the town of Sunderland, and in the year of 1883,
That about 200 children were launch'd into eternity
While witnessing an entertainment in Victoria Hall,
While they, poor little innocents, to God for help did call.

The entertainment consisted of conjuring, and the ghost
    illusion play,
Also talking waxworks, and living marionettes, and given
    by Mr. Fay;
And on this occasion, presents were to be given away,
But in their anxiety of getting presents they wouldn't
    brook delay,
And that is the reason why so many lives have been taken
    away;
But I hope their precious souls are in heaven to-day.

As soon as the children began to suspect
That they would lose their presents by neglect,
They rush'd from the gallery, and ran down the stairs
    pell-mell,
And trampled one another to death, according as they fell.

As soon as the catastrophe became known throughout the
    boro'
The people's hearts were brim-full of sorrow,
And parents rush'd to the Hall terror-stricken and wild,
And each one was anxious to find their own child.

Oh! it must have been a most horrible sight
To see the dear little children struggling with all their
    might
To get out at the door at the foot of the stair,
While one brave little boy did repeat the Lord's Prayer.

The innocent children were buried seven or eight layers
    deep,
The sight was heart-rending and enough to make one weep;
It was a most affecting spectacle and frightful to behold
The corpse of a little boy not above four years old,

Who had on a top-coat much too big for him,
And his little innocent face was white and grim,
And appearing to be simply in a calm sleep—
The sight was enough to make one's flesh to creep.

The scene in the Hall was heart-sickening to behold,
And enough to make one's blood run cold.
To see the children's faces, blackened, that were trampled
    to death,
And their parents lamenting o'er them with bated breath.

Oh! it was most lamentable for to hear
The cries of the mothers for their children dear;
And many mothers swooned in grief away
At the sight of their dead children in grim array.

There was a parent took home a boy by mistake,
And after arriving there his heart was like to break
When it was found to be the body of a neighbour's child;
The parent stood aghast and was like to go wild.

A man and his wife rush'd madly in the Hall,
And loudly in grief on their children they did call,
And the man searched for his children among the dead
Seemingly without the least fear or dread.

And with his finger pointing he cried. "That's one! two!
Oh! heaven above, what shall I do;"
And still he kept walking on and murmuring very low,
Until he came to the last child in the row;

Then he cried, "Good God! all my family gone
And now I am left to mourn alone;"
And staggering back he cried, "Give me water, give me
    water!"
While his heart was like to break and his teeth seem'd to
    chatter.

Oh, heaven! it must have been most pitiful to see
Fathers with their dead children upon their knee
While the blood ran copiously from their mouths and ears
And their parents shedding o'er them hot burning tears.

I hope the Lord will comfort their parents by night and by
    day,
For He gives us life and He takes it away,
Therefore I hope their parents will put their trust in Him,
Because to weep for the dead it is a sin.

Her Majesty's grief for the bereaved parents has been
   profound,
And I'm glad to see that she has sent them £50;
And I hope from all parts of the world will flow relief
To aid and comfort the bereaved parents in their grief.

THE INAUGURATION OF THE UNIVERSITY
COLLEGE, DUNDEE

Good people of Dundee, your voices raise,
And to Miss Baxter give great praise;
Rejoice and sing and dance with glee,
Because she has founded a College in Bonnie Dundee.

Therefore loudly in her praise sing,
And make Dundee with your voices ring,
And give honour to whom honour is due,
Because ladies like her are very few.

'Twas on the 5th day of October, in the year of 1883,
That the University College was opened in Dundee,
And the opening proceedings were conducted in the College
   Hall,
In the presence of ladies and gentlemen both great and small.

Worthy Provost Moncur presided over the meeting,
And received very great greeting;
And Professor Stuart made an eloquent speech there,
And also Lord Dalhousie, I do declare.

Also, the Right Hon W. E. Baxter was there on behalf of
  his aunt,
And acknowledged her beautiful portrait without any rant,
And said that she requested him to hand it over to the
  College,
As an incentive to others to teach the ignorant masses
  knowledge,

Success to Miss Baxter, and praise to the late Doctor Baxter,
  John Boyd,
For I think the Dundonians ought to feel overjoyed
For their munificent gifts to the town of Dundee,
Which will cause their names to be handed down to
  posterity.

The College is most handsome and magnificent to be seen,
And Dundee can now almost cope with Edinburgh or
  Aberdeen,
For the ladies of Dundee can now learn useful knowledge
By going to their own beautiful College.

I hope the ladies and gentlemen of Dundee will try and
  learn knowledge
At home in Dundee in their nice little College,
Because knowledge is sweeter than honey or jam,
Therefore let them try and gain knowledge as quick as they
  can.

It certainly is a great boon and an honour to Dundee
To have a College in our midst, which is most charming to
  see,
All through Miss Baxter and the late Dr Baxter, John Boyd,
Which I hope by the people of Dundee will long be enjoyed.

Now since Miss Baxter has lived to see it erected,
I hope by the students she will long be respected
For establishing a College in Bonnie Dundee,
Where learning can be got of a very high degree.

"My son, get knowledge," so said the sage,
For it will benefit you in your old age,
And help you through this busy world to pass,
For remember a man without knowledge is just like an ass.

I wish the Professors and teachers every success,
Hoping the Lord will all their labours bless;
And I hope the students will always be obedient to their
    teachers,
And that many of them may learn to be orators and
    preachers.

I hope Miss Baxter will prosper for many a long day
For the money that she has given away,
May God shower his blessings on her wise head,
And may all good angels guard her while living and
    hereafter when dead.

THE GREAT FRANCHISE DEMONSTRATION, DUNDEE, 20th SEPTEMBER 1884

'Twas in the year of 1884, and on Saturday the 20th of
    September,
Which the inhabitants of Dundee will long remember
The great Liberal Franchise Demonstration,
Which filled their minds with admiration.

Oh! it was a most magnificent display,
To see about 20 or 30 thousand men all in grand array;
And each man with a medal on his breast;
And every man in the procession dressed in his best.

The banners of the processionists were really grand to see—
The like hasn't been seen for a long time in Dundee;
While sweet music from the bands did rend the skies,
And every processionist was resolved to vote for the
 Franchise.

And as the procession passed along each street,
The spectators did loudly the processionists greet;
As they viewed their beautiful banners waving in the wind,
They declared such a scene would be ever fresh in their
 mind.

The mustering of the processionists was very grand,
As along the Esplanade each man took his stand,
And as soon as they were marshalled in grand array,
To the Magdalen Green, in haste, they wended their way.

And when they arrived on the Magdalen Green,
I'm sure it was a very beautiful imposing scene—
While the cheers of that vast multitude ascended to the
 skies,
For the "Grand Old Man," Gladstone, the Hero of the
 Franchise,

Who has struggled very hard for the people's rights,
Many long years, and many weary nights;
And I think the "Grand Old Man" will gain the Franchise,
And if he does, the people will laud him to the skies.

And his name should be written in letters of gold :
For he is a wise statesman—true and bold—
Who has advocated the people's rights for many long years;
And when he is dead they will thank him with their tears.

For he is the man for the working man,
And without fear of contradiction, deny it who can;
Because he wishes the working man to have a good coat,
And, both in town and country, to have power to vote.

The reason why the Lords wont pass the Franchise Bill :
They fear that it will do themselves some ill;
That is the reason why they wish to throw it out,
Yes, believe me, fellow citizens, that's the cause without
    doubt.

The emblems and mottoes in the procession, were really
    grand,
The like hasn't been seen in broad Scotland;
Especially the picture of Gladstone—the nation's hope,
Who is a much cleverer man than Sir John Cope.

There were masons and ploughmen all in a row,
Also tailors, tenters, and blacksmiths, which made a grand
    show;
Likewise carters and bakers which was most beautiful to be
    seen,
To see them marching from the Esplanade to the Magdalen
    Green.

I'm sure it was a most beautiful sight to see,
The like has never been seen before in Dundee;
Such a body of men, and Gladstone at the helm,
Such a sight, I'm sure, 'twould the Lords o'erwhelm.

Oh! it was grand to see that vast crowd,
And to hear the speeches, most eloquent and loud,
That were made by the speakers, regarding the Franchise;
While the spectators applauded them to the skies.

And for the "Grand Old Man" they gave three cheers,
Hoping he would live for many long years;
And when the speeches were ended, the people's hearts were
    gay,
And they all dispersed quietly to their homes without delay.

THE WRECK OF THE BARQUE "LYNTON" WHILE BOUND FOR ASPINWALL, HAVING ON BOARD 1000 TONS OF COAL

A sad tale of the sea, I will unfold,
About Mrs Lingard, that Heroine bold;
Who struggled hard in the midst of the hurricane wild,
To save herself from being drowned, and her darling child.

'Twas on the 8th of September, the Barque "Lynton"
    sailed for Aspinwall,
And the crew on board, numbered thirteen in all;
And the weather at the time, was really very fine,
On the morning that the ill-fated vessel left the Tyne.

And on the 19th of November, they hove in sight of
    Aspinwall,
But little did they think there was going to be a squall;
When all on a sudden, the sea came rolling in,
And a sound was heard in the heavens, of a rather peculiar
    din.

Then the vivid lightning played around them, and the
    thunder did roar,
And the rain came pouring down, and lashed the barque all
    o'er;
Then the Captain's Wife and Children were ordered below,
And every one on board began to run to and fro.

Then the hurricane in all its fury, burst upon them,
And the sea in its madness, washed the deck from stem to
    stem;
And the rain poured in torrents, and the waves seemed
    mountains high,
Then all on board the barque, to God for help, did loudly
    cry.

And still the wind blew furiously, and the darkness was
    intense,
Which filled the hearts of the crew with great suspense,
Then the ill-fated vessel struck, and began to settle down,
Then the poor creatures cried, God save us, or else we'll
    drown!

Then Mrs Lingard snatched to her breast, her darling child,
While loudly roared the thunder, and the hurricane wild;
And she cried, oh! God of heaven, save me and my darling
    child,
Or else we'll perish in the hurricane wild.

'Twas then the vessel turned right over, and they were
    immersed in the sea,
Still the poor souls struggled hard to save their lives, most
    heroically;
And everyone succeeded in catching hold of the keel
    garboard streak,
While with cold and fright, their hearts were like to break.

Not a word or a shriek came from Mrs Lingard, the Captain's
    wife,
While she pressed her child to her bosom, as dear she loved
    her life;
Still the water dashed over them again and again,
And about one o'clock, the boy, Hall, began to complain.

Then Mrs Lingard put his cold hands into her bosom,
To warm them because with cold he was almost frozen,
And at the same time clasping her child Hilda to her breast,
While the poor boy Hall closely to her prest.

And there the poor creatures lay huddled together with
    fear,
And the weary night seemed to them more like a year,
And they saw the natives kindling fires on the shore,
To frighten wild animals away, that had begun to roar.

Still the big waves broke over them, which caused them to
    exclaim,
Oh! God, do thou save us for we are suffering pain;
But, alas, the prayers they uttered were all in vain,
Because the boy Hall and Jonson were swept from the
    wreck and never rose again.

Then bit by bit the vessel broke up, and Norberg was swept
    away,
Which filled the rest of the survivors hearts with great
    dismay;
But at length the longed for morning dawned at last,
Still with hair streaming in the wind, Mrs Lingard to the
    wreck held fast.

Then Captain Lingard still held on with Lucy in his arms,
Endeavouring to pacify the child from the storms alarms;
And at last the poor child's spirits began to sink,
And she cried in pitiful accents, papa! papa! give me a
   drink.

And in blank amazement the Captain looked all round
   about,
And he cried Lucy dear I cannot find you a drink I doubt,
Unless my child God sends it to you,
Then he sank crying Lucy, my dear child, and wife, adieu!
   adieu!

'Twas then a big wave swept Lucy and the Carpenter away,
Which filled Mrs Lingard's heart with great dismay,
And she cried Mr Jonson my dear husband and child are
   gone,
But still she held to the wreck while the big waves rolled on.

For about 38 hours they suffered on the wreck,
At length they saw a little boat which seemed like a speck,
Making towards them on the top of a wave,
Buffetting with the billows fearlessly and brave.

And when the boat to them drew near,
Poor souls they gave a feeble cheer,
While the hurricane blew loud and wild,
Yet the crew succeeded in saving Mrs Lingard and her
   child.

Also, the Steward and two sailors named Christophers and
    Eversen,
Able-bodied and expert brave seamen.
And they were all taken to a French Doctor's and attended
    to,
And they caught the yellow fever, but the Lord brought
    them through.

And on the 6th of December they embarked on board the
    ship Moselle,
All in high spirits, and in health very well,
And arrived at Southampton on the 29th of December,
A day which the survivors will long remember.

THE GREAT YELLOW RIVER INUNDATION
IN CHINA

'Twas in the year of 1887, and on the 28th of September,
Which many people of Honan, in China, will long
    remember;
Especially those that survived the mighty deluge,
That fled to the mountains, and tops of trees, for refuge.

The river burst its embankments suddenly at dead of night,
And the rushing torrent swept all before it left and right;
All over the province of Honan, which for its fertility,
Is commonly called by historians, the garden of China.

The river was at its fullest when the embankment gave way,
And when the people heard it, oh! horror and dismay;
'Twas then fathers and mothers leaped from their beds
    without delay,
And some saved themselves from being drowned, but
    thousands were swept away.

95

Oh! it was a horrible and most pitiful scene,
To hear fathers and mothers and their children loudly
    scream;
As the merciless water encircled their bodies around,
While the water spirits laughed to see them drowned.

Oh! heaven, it must have been an appalling sight,
To witness in the dead stillness of the night
Frantic fathers and mothers, struggling hard against the
    roaring flood,
To save themselves and little ones, their own flesh and
    blood.

The watchmen tried to patch the breach, but it was all in
    vain,
Because the banks were sodden with the long prolonged
    rain;
And driven along by a high wind, which brought the last
    strain,
Which caused the water with resistless fury to spread o'er
    the plain.

And the torrent poured into the valley of the La Chia river,
Sweeping thousands of the people before it ere a helping
    hand could them deliver;
Oh! it was horrible to hear the crashing of houses fallen on
    every side,
As the flood of rushing waters spread far and wide.

The Chinese offer sacrifices to the water spirits twice a year,
And whether the water spirits or God felt angry I will not
    aver;
But perhaps God has considered such sacrifices a sin,
And has drowned so many thousands of them for not
    worshipping Him.

How wonderful are the **works of God,**
At times among His people abroad;
Therefore, let us be careful of what we do or say,
For fear God doth suddenly take our lives away.

The province of Honan is about half the size of Scotland,
Dotted over with about 3000 villages, most grand;
And inhabited by millions of people of every degree,
And these villages, and people were transformed into a
  raging sea.

The deluge swept on over the fertile and well-cultivated
  land,
And the rushing of the mighty torrent no power could
  withstand;
And the appalling torrent was about twenty feet deep,
And with resistless fury everything before it it did sweep.

Methinks I see the waste of surging waters, and hear its
  deafening roar,
And on its surface I see corpses of men and women by the
  score;
And the merciless torrent in the darkness of the night,
Sportively tossing them about, oh! what a horrible sight.

Besides there were buffaloes and oxen, timber, straw, and
  grain,
Also three thousand villages were buried beneath the waters
  of the plain;
And multitudes beneath their own roofs have found a
  watery grave,
While struggling hard, no doubt, poor souls their lives to
  save.

Therefore good people at home or abroad,
Be advised by me and trust more in God,
Than the people of Honan, the benighted Chinese,
For fear God punished you likewise for your iniquities.

THE DEATH OF FRED. MARSDEN, THE AMERICAN PLAYWRIGHT

A pathetic tragedy I will relate,
Concerning poor Fred. Marsden's fate,
Who suffocated himself by the fumes of gas,
On the 18th of May, and in the year of 1888, alas!

Fred. Marsden was a playwright, the theatrical world
    knows,
And was highly esteemed by the people, and had very few
    foes;
And in New York, in his bedroom, he took his life away,
And was found by his servant William in his bedroom where
    he lay.

The manner in which he took his life : first he locked the
    door,
Then closed down the window, and a sheet to shreds he tore,
And then stopped the keyholes and chinks through which
    air might come,
Then turned on the single gas-burner, and soon the deed
    was done.

About seven o'clock in the evening he bade his wife
good-night,
And she left him, smoking, in his room, thinking all was
right,
But when morning came his daughter said she smelled gas,
Then William, his servant, called loudly on him, but no
answer, alas!

Then suspicion flashed across William's brain, and he broke
open the door,
Then soon the family were in a state of uproar,
For the room was full of gas, and Mr Marsden quite dead,
And a more kind-hearted father never ate of the world's
bread.

And by his kindness he spoiled his only child,
His pretty daughter Blanche, which made him wild;
For some time he thought her an angel, she was so very
civil,
But she dishonoured herself, and proved herself a devil.

Her father idolised her, and on her spared no expense,
And the kind-hearted father gave her too much indulgence,
Because evening parties and receptions were got up for her
sake,
Besides, he bought her a steam yacht to sail on Schroon
Lake.

His means he lavished upon his home and his wife,
And he loved his wife and daughter as dear as his life;
But Miss Blanche turned to folly, and wrecked their home
through strife,
And through Miss Marsden's folly her father took his life.

She wanted to ride, and her father bought her a horse,
And by giving her such indulgences, in morals she grew
  worse;
And by her immoral actions she broke her father's heart;
And, in my opinion, she has acted a very ungrateful part.

At last she fled from her father's house, which made him
  mourn,
Then the crazy father went after her and begged her to
  return,
But she tore her father's beard, and about the face beat
  him,
Then fled to her companions in evil, and thought it no sin.

Then her father sent her one hundred dollars, and found her
  again,
And he requested her to come home, but it was all in vain;
For his cruel daughter swore at him without any dread,
And, alas! next morning, he was found dead in his bed.

And soon theatrical circles were shocked to learn,
Of the sudden death of genial Fred. Marsden,
Whose house had been famous for its hospitality,
To artists, litterateurs, and critics of high and low degree.

And now dear Mrs Marsden is left alone to mourn
The loss of her loving husband, whom to her will ne'er
  return;
But I hope God will be kind to her in her bereavement,
And open her daughter's eyes, and make her repent

For being the cause of her father's death, the generous **Fred**,
Who oft poor artists and mendicants has fed;
But, alas! his bounties they will never receive more,
Therefore poor artists and mendicants will his loss
   deplore.

Therefore, all ye kind parents of high and low degree,
I pray ye all, be advised by me,
And never pamper your children in any way,
Nor idolise them, for they are apt to go astray,

And treat ye, like pretty Blanche Marsden,
Who by her folly has been the death of one of the finest
   men;
So all kind parents, be warned by me,
And remember always this sad Tragedy!

AN EXCURSION STEAMER SUNK IN THE TAY

'Twas in the year of 1888, and on July the 14th day,
That an alarming accident occurred in the River Tay.
Which resulted in the sinking of the Tay Ferries' Steamer
   "Dundee,"
Which was a most painful and sickening sight to see.

The Steamer was engaged by the Independent Order of
   Rechabites,
And all were resolved to see some rural sights;
And the place they selected was the village of Newburgh;
While each heart was happy and free from sorrow.

And the weather was sunny, and really very fine,
And 900 souls had agreed to while away the time;
And they left the Craig Pier at half-past two o'clock,
Never thinking they would meet with an accidental
  shock.

And after passing underneath the Bridge of Tay,
Then they took the Channel on the south side without
  dismay;
And Captain Methven stood on the Steamer's bridge, I do
  declare,
And for the passengers he seemed to have very great care.

And all went well on board for some time,
And the silvery Tay shone beautiful in the sunshine;
And the passengers' hearts felt light and gay,
While they gazed on the bonnie banks of the silvery Tay.

To do justice to the passengers, they were a goodly band,
For their behaviour, 'tis said, was truly grand;
But to the eastward of Newburgh, the Steamer was too close
  inshore,
And on passing a boatman, he warningly to them did roar,—

Warning them not to come inshore so near,
But his warning voice the helmsman didn't hear;
Neither the Captain or passengers his warning dreads,
Until the Steamer struck a number of boulders, known as
  The Heads.

And close to the point where the Pow falls into the Tay,
Which the people that escaped drowning will remember for
  many a day,
Because many of the passengers were thrown off their
  balance;
But, most fortunately, they were all saved merely by
  chance.

And owing to the suddenness of the shock, many women
  fainted away,
Which filled the rest of the passengers' hearts with dismay;
But they soon regained their composure when close to the
  land,
Especially when they saw that succour was near at hand.

The engines were kept going at full speed,
And God helped His people in time of need;
And in a short time Newburgh was reached,
While many women wept bitterly, and loudly screeched.

Because by this time the forehold was nearly filled with
  water,
Which caused the passengers' teeth with fear to chatter;
Because the Steamer was settling down forward,
While to land the passengers safe Captain Methven struggled
  hard.

But before one-half of them had got ashore,
The women and children were in a state of uproar,
Because the forepart of the Steamer was submerged in the
  Tay,
Which filled the passengers' hearts with dismay.

But, thanks be to God! all the passengers were sent to
Dundee
By the Steamers Renown, Forfarshire, Protector, and the
Lass o' Gowrie,
Which certainly was a most beautiful sight to see,
When they landed 900 passengers safe on the pier at
Dundee.

Then, good people, away to the mountains, glens, and lakes,
And drink of milk and pure water, and eat oaten cakes;
And sit down on the margin of a little burn in the sunshine,
And enjoy yourselves heartily during the holiday time.

THE FUNERAL OF THE LATE EX-PROVOST
ROUGH, DUNDEE

'Twas in the year of 1888, and on the 19th of November,
Which the friends of the late Ex-Provost Rough will long
remember,
Because 'twas on the 19th of November his soul took its
flight
To the happy land above, the land of pure delight.

Take him for all in all, he was a very good man,
And during his Provostship he couldn't be equalled in
Great Britain,
Which I proclaim to the world without any dread,
Because while Provost he reduced the public-houses to
three hundred.

Whereas at the time there were 620 public-houses in the
   town,
But being a friend of the temperance cause he did frown,
Because he saw the evils of intemperance every day
While sitting on the bench, so he resolved to sweep public-
   houses away.

And in doing so the good man, in my opinion, was right,
Because the evils of intemperance is an abomination in
   God's sight;
And all those that get drunk are enemies to Him,
Likewise enemies to Christ's kingdom, which is a great sin.

The late Ex-Provost Rough was President of the Dundee
   Temperance Society,
An office which he filled with great ability;
Besides Vice-President of the Scottish Temperance League
   for many years,
And no doubt the friends of temperance for his loss will
   shed tears.

Because many a hungry soul he relieved while in distress,
And for doing so I hope the Lord will him bless,
For his kindness towards the poor people in Dundee,
Besides for his love towards the temperance cause, and his
   integrity.

And when the good man's health began to decline
The doctor ordered him to take each day two glasses of
   wine,
But he soon saw the evil of it, and from it he shrunk,
The noble old patriarch, for fear of getting drunk.

And although the doctor advised him to continue taking the
  wine,
Still the hero of the temperance cause did decline,
And told the doctor he wouldn't of wine take any
  more,
So in a short time his spirit fled to heaven, where all
  troubles are o'er.

I'm sure very little good emanates from strong drink,
And many people, alas! it leads to hell's brink!
Some to the scaffold, and some to a pauper's grave,
Whereas if they would abstain from drink, Christ would
  them save.

'Twas on Friday afternoon, in November the 23rd day,
That the funeral cortege to the Western Cemetery wended
  its way,
Accompanied by the Magistrates, and amongst those
  present were—
Bailie Macdonald and Bailie Black, also Lord Provost
  Hunter I do declare.

There were also Bailie Foggie, Bailie Craig, and Bailie
  Stephenson,
And Ex-Provost Moncur, and Ex-Provost Ballingall
  representing the Royal Orphan Institution;
Besides there were present the Rev. J. Jenkins and the Rev.
  J. Masson,
With grief depicted in their faces and seemingly
  woe-begone.

There were also Mr Henry Adams, representing the Glover
    trade,
Also Mr J. Carter, who never was afraid
To denounce strong drink, and to warn the people from it
    to flee,
While agent of the Temperance Society in Dundee.

And when the funeral cortege arrived at the Western
    burying-ground,
Then the clergyman performed the funeral service with a
    solemn sound;
While from the eyes of the spectators fell many a tear
For the late Ex-Provost Rough they loved so dear.

And when the coffin was lowered into its house of clay,
Then the friends of the deceased homewards wended their
    way,
Conversing on the good qualities of the good man,
Declaring that the late Ex-Provost Rough couldn't be
    equalled in Great Britain.

THE CRUCIFIXION OF CHRIST
COMPOSED, BY SPECIAL REQUEST, 18TH JUNE 1890

Then Pilate, the Roman Governor, took Jesus and scourged
    Him,
And the soldiers platted a crown of thorns, and thought it
    no sin
To put it on His head, while meekly Jesus stands;
They put on Him a purple robe, and smote Him with their
    hands.

Then Pilate went forth again, and said unto them,
Behold, I bring Him forth to you, but I cannot Him
  condemn,
And I would have you to remember I find no fault in Him,
And to treat Him too harshly 'twould be a sin.

But the rabble cried, Hail, King of the Jews, and crucify
  Him;
But Pilate saith unto them, I find in Him no sin;
Then Jesus came forth, looking dejected and wan,
And Pilate saith unto them, Behold the Man.

Then the Jews cried out, By our laws He ought to die,
Because He made Himself the Son of God the Most High;
And when Pilate heard that saying the Jews had made,
He saw they were dissatisfied, and he was the more afraid.

And to release Jesus Pilate did really intend,
But the Jews cried angrily, Pilate, thou art not Caesar's
  friend,
Remember, if thou let this vile impostor go,
It only goes to prove thou art Caesar's foe.

When Pilate heard that he felt very irate,
Then he brought Jesus forth, and sat down in the
  judgment-seat,
In a place that is called the Pavement,
While the Blessed Saviour stood calm and content.

The presence of His enemies did not Him appal,
When Pilate asked of Him, before them all,
Whence art Thou, dost say from on High ?
But Jesus, the Lamb of God, made no reply.

Then saith Pilate unto Him, Speakest Thou not unto me,
Remember, I have the power to crucify Thee;
But Jesus answered, Thou hast no power at all against me,
Except from above it were given to thee.

Then Pilate to the Jews loudly cried,
Take Him away to be crucified;
Then the soldiers took Jesus and led Him away,
And He, bearing His Cross, without dismay.

And they led Him to a place called Golgotha,
But the Saviour met His fate without any awe,
And there crucified Him with two others, one on either side,
And Jesus in the midst, whilst the Jews did Him deride.

Then Pilate tried to pacify the Jews, they felt so morose,
And he wrote a title, and put it on the Cross;
And the title he wrote did the Jews amuse,
The writing was, Jesus of Nazareth the King of the Jews.

This title read many of the Jews without any pity;
And the place where Jesus was crucified was nigh to the
    city;
And the title was written in Hebrew, and Greek, and Latin,
And while reading the title the Jews did laugh and grin.

While on the Cross the sun refused to shine,
And there was total darkness for a long time;
The reason was God wanted to hide His wounds from view,
And He kept the blessed sun from breaking through.

And to quench His thirst they gave Him vinegar and
hyssop,
While the blood from His wounded brow copiously did
drop,
Then He drank of it willingly, and bowed His head,
And in a few minutes the dear Saviour was dead.

Then Joseph of Arimathea sadly did grieve,
And he asked if Pilate would give him leave
To take the body of Jesus away,
And Pilate told him to remove it without delay.

Then Joseph took the body of Jesus away,
And wound it in linen, which was the Jewish custom of
that day,
And embalmed his body with spices sweet,
Then laid it in a new sepulchre, as Joseph thought meet.

But death could not hold Him in the grave,
Because He died poor sinners' souls to save;
And God His Father took Him to Heaven on high;
And those that believe in Jesus shall never die.

Oh! think of the precious Blood our Saviour did loss,
That flowed from His wounds while on the Cross,
Especially the wound in His side, made with a spear,
And if you are a believer, you will drop a silent tear.

And if you are not a believer, try and believe,
And don't let the devil any longer you deceive,
Because the precious Blood that Jesus shed will free you
from all sin,
Therefore, believe in the Saviour, and Heaven you shall
enter in!

DEATH AND BURIAL OF LORD TENNYSON

Alas! England now mourns for her poet that's gone—
The late and the good Lord Tennyson.
I hope his soul has fled to heaven above,
Where there is everlasting joy and love.

He was a man that didn't care for company,
Because company interfered with his study,
And confused the bright ideas in his brain,
And for that reason from company he liked to abstain.

He has written some fine pieces of poetry in his time,
Especially the May Queen, which is really sublime;
Also the gallant charge of the Light Brigade—
A most heroic poem, and beautifully made.

He believed in the Bible, also in Shakspeare,
Which he advised young men to read without any fear;
And by following the advice of both works therein,
They would seldom or never commit any sin.

Lord Tennyson's works are full of the scenery of his
    boyhood,
And during his life all his actions were good;
And Lincolnshire was closely associated with his history,
And he has done what Wordsworth did for the Lake
    Country.

His remains now rest in Westminster Abbey,
And his funeral was very impressive to see;
It was a very touching sight, I must confess,
Every class, from the Queen, paying a tribute to the poet's
    greatness.

The pall-bearers on the right of the coffin were Mr W. E. H.
    Lecky,
And Professor Butler, Master of Trinity, and the Earl of
    Rosebery;
And on the left were Mr J. A. Froude and the Marquis of
    Salisbury,
Also Lord Selborne, which was an imposing sight to see.

There were also on the left Professor Jowett,
Besides Mr Henry Whyte and Sir James Paget,
And the Marquis of Dufferin and the Duke of Argyll,
And Lord Salisbury, who seemed melancholy all the while.

The chief mourners were all of the Tennyson family,
Including the Hon. Mr and Mrs Hallam Tennyson, and
    Masters Lionel and Aubrey,
And Mr Arthur Tennyson, and Mr and Mrs Horatio
    Tennyson;
Also Sir Andrew Clark, who was looking woe begone.

The bottom of the grave was thickly strewn with white
    roses,
And for such a grave kings will sigh where the poet now
    reposes;
And many of the wreaths were much observed and
    commented upon,
And conspicuous amongst them was one from Mrs
    Gladstone.

The Gordon boys were there looking solemn and serene,
Also Sir Henry Ponsonby to represent the Queen,
Likewise Henry Irving, the great tragedian,
With a solemn aspect, and driving his brougham.

And, in conclusion, I most earnestly pray,
That the people will erect a monument for him without
   delay,
To commemorate the good work he has done,
And his name in gold letters written thereon!

A NEW YEAR'S RESOLUTION TO LEAVE DUNDEE

Welcome! thrice welcome! to the year 1893,
For it is the year that I intend to leave Dundee,
Owing to the treatment I receive,
Which does my heart sadly grieve.
Every morning when I go out
The ignorant rabble they do shout
'There goes Mad McGonagall'
In derisive shouts, as loud as they can bawl,
And lifts stones and snowballs, throws them at me;
And such actions are shameful to be heard in the City of
   Dundee.
And I'm ashamed, kind Christians, to confess,
That from the Magistrates I can get no redress.
Therefore I have made up my mind, in the year of
   1893,
To leave the Ancient City of Dundee,
Because the citizens and me cannot agree.
The reason why ?—because they disrespect me,
Which makes me feel rather discontent.
Therefore, to leave them I am bent;
And I will make my arrangements without delay,
And leave Dundee some early day.

LINES IN REPLY TO THE BEAUTIFUL POET, WHO WELCOMED NEWS OF McGONAGALL'S DEPARTURE FROM DUNDEE

Dear Johnny, I return my thanks to you;
But more than thanks is your due
For publishing the scurrilous poetry about me
Leaving the Ancient City of Dundee.

The rhymster says, we'll weary for your schauchlin' form;
But if I'm not mistaken I've seen bonnier than his in a field
  of corn;
And, as I venture to say and really suppose,
His form seen in a cornfield would frighten the crows.

But, dear Johnny, as you said, he's just a lampoon,
And as ugly and as ignorant as a wild baboon;
And, as far as I can judge or think,
He is a vendor of strong drink.

He says my nose would make a peasemeal warrior weep;
But I've seen a much bonnier sweep,
And a more manly and wiser man
Than he is by far, deny it who can!

And, in conclusion, I'd have him to beware,
And never again to interfere with a poet's hair,
Because Christ the Saviour wore long hair,
And many more good men, I do declare.

Therefore I laugh at such bosh that appears in print.
So I hope from me you will take the hint,
And never publish such bosh of poetry again,
Or else you'll get the famous *Weekly News* a bad name.

LINES IN MEMORIAM REGARDING THE ENTERTAINMENT I GAVE ON THE 31st MARCH, 1893, IN REFORM STREET HALL, DUNDEE

'Twas on the 31st of March, and in the year of 1893,
I gave an entertainment in the city of Dundee,
To a select party of gentlemen, big and small,
Who appreciated my recital in Reform Street Hall.

The meeting was convened by J. P. Smith's manager,
   High Street,
And many of J. P. Smith's employes were there me to
   greet,
And several other gentlemen within the city,
Who were all delighted with the entertainment they got
   from me.

Mr Green was the chairman for the night,
And in that capacity he acted right;
He made a splendid address on my behalf,
Without introducing any slang or chaff.

I wish him success during life;
May he always feel happy and free from strife,
For the kindness he has ever shown to me
During our long acquaintance in Dundee.

I return my thanks to Mr J. P. Smith's men,
Who were at my entertainment more than nine or ten;
And the rest of the gentlemen that were there,
Also deserves my thanks, I do declare.

Because they showered upon me their approbation,
And got up for me a handsome donation,
Which was presented to me by Mr Green,
In a purse most beautiful to be seen.

Which was a generous action in deed,
And came to me in time of need.
And the gentlemen that so generously treated me
I'll remember during my stay in Dundee.

LINES IN PRAISE OF MR J. GRAHAM HENDERSON, HAWICK

Success to Mr J. Graham Henderson, who is a good man,
And to gainsay it there's few people can,
I say so from my own experience,
And experience is a great defence.

He is a good man, I venture to say,
Which I declare to the world without dismay,
Because he's given me a suit of Tweeds, magnificent to
  see,
So good that it cannot be surpassed in Dundee.

The suit is the best of Tweed cloth in every way,
And will last me for many a long day;
It's really good, and in no way bad,
And will help to make my heart feel glad.

He's going to send some goods to the World's Fair,
And I hope of patronage he will get the biggest share;
Because his Tweed cloth is the best I ever did see,
In the year of our Lord eighteen hundred and ninety-three.

At the International Exhibition, and the Isle of Man
    Exhibition,
He got a gold medal from each, in recognition
Of his Scotch Tweeds, so good and grand,
Which cannot be surpassed in fair Scotland.

Therefore, good people, his goods are really grand,
And manufactured at Weensforth Mill, Hawick, Scotland;
Where there's always plenty of Tweeds on hand,
For the ready cash at the people's command.

Mr Tocher measured me for the suit,
And it is very elegant, which no one will dispute,
And I hope Mr Henry in Reform Street
Will gain customers by it, the suit is so complete.

THE TERRIFIC CYCLONE OF 1893

'Twas in the year of 1893, and on the 17th and 18th of
    November,
Which the people of Dundee and elsewhere will long
    remember,
The terrific cyclone that blew down trees,
And wrecked many vessels on the high seas.

All along the coast the Storm Fiend did loudly roar,
Whereby many ships were wrecked along the shore,
And many seamen lost their lives,
Which caused their children to mourn and their wives.

Alas! they will never see their husbands again,
And to weep for them 'tis all in vain,
Because sorrow never could revive the dead,
Therefore they must weep, knowing all hope is fled.

The people's hearts in Dundee were full of dread
For fear of chimney-cans falling on their heads,
And the roofs of several houses were hurled to the ground,
And the tenants were affrighted, and their sorrow was
   profound,

And scores of wooden sheds were levelled to the ground,
And chimney stalks fell with a crashing rebound :
The gale swept everything before it in its way;
No less than 250 trees and 37 tombstones were blown down
   at Balgay.

Oh! it was a pitiful and a terrible sight
To see the fallen trees lying left and right,
Scattered about in the beautiful Hill of Balgay,
Also the tombstones that were swept away.

At Broughty Ferry the gale made a noise like thunder,
Which made the inhabitants shake with fear and wonder
If their dwellings would be blown to the ground,
While the slates and chimney-cans were falling all around.

Early on the 18th a disaster occurred on the Tay :
The wreck of the steamer "Union,"—Oh! horror and
   dismay!
Whereby four lives have been taken away,
Which will make their friends mourn for many a day.

The steamer left Newburgh for Dundee with a cargo of
    sand,
And the crew expected they would safely land,
But by the time the steamer was opposite Dundee,
Alas! stronger blew the gale, and heavier grew the sea.

And in order to prevent stranding the anchor was let go,
And with the cold the hearts of the crew were full of woe,
While the merciless Storm Fiend loudly did roar,
As the vessel was driven towards the Fife shore.

Then the crew took shelter in the stokehole,
From the cold wind they could no longer thole,
But the high seas broke over her, one finding its way
Right into the stokehole, which filled the crew's hearts with
    dismay.

Then one of the crew, observing that the steamer had
    broached to,
Immediately went on deck to see what he could do,
And he tried hard to keep her head to the sea,
But the big waves dashed over her furiously.

Then Strachan shouted that the "Union" was sinking fast,
Which caused his companions to stand aghast,
And Strachan tried to lower the small boat,
But alas! the vessel sunk, and the boat wouldn't float,

And before he could recover himself he was struggling in the
    sea,
And battling with the big waves right manfully,
But his companions sank with the "Union" in the Tay,
Which filled Strachan's heart with sorrow and dismay,

And after a great struggle he reached the beach,
Fortunately so, which he never expected to reach,
For often he was drawn back by the back-wash,
As the big waves against his body did dash.

But, when nearly exhausted, and near to the land,
A piece of wreckage was near him, which he grasped with
  his hand,
Which providentially came within his reach,
And bruised, and battered, he was thrown on the
  beach.

He was so exhausted, he was unable to stand upright,
He felt so weakly, he was in such a plight,
Because the big waves had done him bodily harm,
Yet on hands and knees he crept to a house at Northfield
  farm.

He arrived there at ten minutes past four o'clock,
And when he awakened the inmates, their nerves got a
  shock,
But under their kind treatment he recovered speedily,
And was able to recount the disaster correctly.

Oh! it was a fearful, and a destructive storm!
I never mind the like since I was born,
Only the Tay Bridge storm of 1879,
And both these storms will be remembered for a very long
  time.

A TRIBUTE TO DR MURISON

Success to the good and skilful Dr Murison,
For golden opinions he has won
From his patients one and all,
And from myself, McGonagall.

He is very skilful and void of pride;
He was so to me when at my bedside,
When I turned badly on the 25th of July,
And was ill with inflammation, and like to die.

He told me at once what was ailing me;
He said I had been writing too much poetry,
And from writing poetry I would have to refrain,
Because I was suffering from inflammation on the brain.

And he has been very good to me in my distress,
Good people of Dundee, I honestly confess,
And to all his patients as well as me
Within the Royal city of Dundee.

He is worthy of the public's support,
And to his shop they should resort
To get his advice one and all;
Believe me on him ye ought to call.

He is very affable in temper and a skilful man,
And to cure all his patients he tries all he can;
And I wish him success for many a long day,
For he has saved me from dying, I venture to say;
The kind treatment I received surpasses all
Is the honest confession of McGonagall.

THE KESSACK FERRY-BOAT FATALITY

'Twas on Friday the 2nd of March in the year of 1894,
That the Storm Fiend did loudly laugh and roar
Along the Black Isle and the Kessack Ferry shore,
Whereby six men were drowned, which their friends will
    deplore.

The accident is the most serious that has occurred for many
    years,
And their relatives no doubt will shed many tears,
Because the accident happened within 200 yards of the
    shore,
While Boreas he did loudly rail and roar.

The ferry-boat started from the north or Black Isle,
While the gusty gales were blowing all the while
From the south, and strong from the south-west,
And to get to land the crew tried their utmost best.

The crew, however, were very near the land,
When the gusts rose such as no man could withstand,
With such force that the ferry-boat flew away
From her course, down into the little bay,

Which opens into the Moray Firth and the river Ness,
And by this time the poor men were in great distress,
And they tried again and again to get back to the pier,
And to save themselves from being drowned they began to
    fear.

And at last the poor men began to despair,
And they decided to drop anchor where they were,
While the Storm Fiend did angry roar,
And the white-crested billows did lash the shore.

And the water poured in, but was baled out quickly,
And the men's clothes were wet, and they felt sickly,
Because they saw no help in the distance,
Until at last they blew the fog-horn for assistance.

And quickly in response to their cry of distress,
Four members of the coastguard, in coastguard dress,
Whose station overlooked the scene, put off in a small boat,
And with a desperate struggle they managed to keep her
    afloat.

Then the coastguards and boat drifted rapidly away,
Until they found themselves in the little bay,
Whilst the big waves washed o'er them, again and again,
And they began to think their struggling was all in vain.

But they struggled on manfully until they came upon a
    smaller boat,
Which they thought would be more easily kept afloat,
And to which the hawser was soon transferred,
Then for a second time to save the ferrymen all was
    prepared.

Then the coastguards drifted down alongside the ferry-boat,
And with great difficulty they kept themselves afloat,
Because the big waves were like mountains high,
Yet the coastguards resolved to save the ferrymen or die.

Then at last the ferrymen got into the coastguard boat,
And they all toiled manfully to keep her afloat,
Until she was struck as she rose on the crest of the wave,
Then each one tried hard his life to save.

And the poor men's hearts with grief were rent,
For they were thrown into the merciless sea in a moment,
And out of the eight men two have been saved,
All owing to their swimming abilities, and how they
    behaved.

Oh! it must have been a fearful sight,
To see them striving hard with all their might
To save themselves from a watery grave,
While the Storm Fiend did laugh and angry did rave.

LINES IN PRAISE OF THE LYRIC CLUB BANQUET, WHICH WAS HELD IN THE QUEEN'S HOTEL, PERTH. ON THE EVENING OF THE 5TH OF SEPTEMBER 1894

'Twas in the year of 1894, and on the 5th of September,
Which for a long time I will remember,
And the gentlemen I entertained in the city of Perth,
Which is one of the grandest cities upon the earth.

At the Banquet there were gentlemen of high degree,
And the viands they partook of filled their hearts with glee;
There was Beef, Fish, and Potatoes galore,
And we all ate until we could eat no more

124

The gentlemen present were very kind to me,
And the entertainment I gave them filled their hearts with
   glee;
Especially the Recital I gave them from "Macbeth",
They were so much fascinated they almost lost their breath.

The audience were orderly and all went well,
As cheerily and as smoothly as a marriage bell.
Mr James Speedie was the chairman, and behaved right
   manfully,
And sang a beautiful song, which filled our hearts with glee.

But when I sang my "Rattling Boy from Dublin Town",
The audience were like to pull the house down
With the hearty applause they showered upon me,
Because I sang the song so merrily.

But, in conclusion, I must honestly say
I haven't been so well treated for many a day;
Because I got a Splendid Bed in the Queen's Hotel,
And the breakfast I got there I liked right well.

The treatment I received there would please the Queen,
Because the cooking is most excellent and the beds are
   clean;
And, in conclusion, I return my thanks to one and all,
Especially the members of the Lyric Club, big and small,
Also the landlord of the Queen's Hotel, yours truly,

McGONAGALL.

LINES IN PRAISE OF PROFESSOR BLACKIE

Alas! the people's hearts are now full of sorrow
For the deceased Professor Blackie, of Edinboro';
Because he was a Christian man, affable and kind,
And his equal in charitable actions would be hard to find

'Twas in the year of 1895, March the 2nd, he died at
    10 o'clock.
Which to his dear wife, and his adopted son, was a great
    shock;
And before he died he bade farewell to his adopted son
    and wife.
Which, no doubt, they will remember during life.

Professor Blackie celebrated his golden wedding three
    years ago,
When he was made the recipient of respect from high and
    low.
He leaves a widow, but, fortunately, no family,
Which will cause Mrs. Blackie to feel less unhappy.

Professor Blackie will be greatly missed in Edinboro;
Especially those that met him daily will feel great sorrow,
When they think of his never-failing plaid and hazel rung,
For, although he was an old man, he considered he was
    young.

He had a very striking face, and silvery locks like a seer,
And in the hearts of the Scottish people he was loved
    most dear;
And many a heart will mourn for him, but all in vain,
Because he never can return to them again.

He was a very kind-hearted man, and in no way vain,
And I'm afraid we ne'er shall look upon his like again;
And to hear him tell Scotch stories, the time did quickly
 pass,
And for singing Scotch songs few could him surpass.

But I hope he is in heaven, singing with saints above,
Around God's throne, where all is peace and love;
There, where God's children daily doth meet
To sing praises to God, enchanting and sweet.

He had visited almost every part of Europe in his time,
And, like Lord Byron, he loved the Grecian clime;
Nor did he neglect his own dear country,
And few men knew it more thoroughly than he.

On foot he tramped o'er most of bonnie Scotland,
And in his seventies he climbed the highest hills most
 grand.
Few men in his day could be compared to him,
Because he wasn't hard on fallen creatures when they did
 sin.

Oh, dearly beloved Professor Blackie, I must conclude my
 muse,
And to write in praise of thee my pen does not refuse;
Because you were a very Christian man, be it told,
Worthy of a monument, and your name written thereon
 in letters of gold.

THE FUNERAL OF THE LATE PRINCE HENRY
OF BATTENBERG

Alas! Prince Henry of Battenberg is dead!
And, I hope, has gone to heaven,its streets to tread,
And to sing with God's saints above,
Where all is joy and peace and love.

'Twas in the year of 1896, and on the 5th of February,
Prince Henry was buried at Whippingham—a solemn
   sight to see.
As the funeral moved off, it was a very impressive sight—
First came the military, and police, and volunteers from
   the Isle of Wight.

Then came the carriage party of the Scots Guards;
While the people uncovered their heads as it passed
   onwards
And many of them did sob and sigh
When the gun carriage with the coffin was passing by.

Prince Henry's charger was led by Richter, his stud groom;
And depicted in the people's faces there was a sad gloom
When they saw the noble charger of the dead—
It seemed that all joy from them had fled.

The Queen's carriage was followed by the Princess of
   Wales, and other Princesses,
All clad in gorgeous mourning dresses;
And there was a number of military representatives, which
   enhanced the scene;
And as the procession moved along it was solemn in the
   extreme.

Her Majesty looked very sad and serene,
Leaning back in her carriage could plainly be seen;
And the carriage was drawn by a pair of greys in grand
  harness;
And Her Majesty seemed to be in deep distress.

By Her Majesty's side sat the Princess Beatrice
And the two younger Battenberg children, looking very
  nice;
And by the coffin walked the elder Prince, immediately
Between Prince Louis and Prince Joseph, holding their
  hands tenderly.

The "Dead March" was played by the Marine Band;
And the music was solemn and very grand,
And accompanied by the roll of muffled drums;
Whilst among the spectators were heard sighs and hums.

And when the procession arrived at the church of
  Whippingham,
Then the coffin was carried inside—of the good man—
And was then laid in its resting place,
While sorrow was depicted in every face.

Then there was the firing of guns, with their earthly
  thunder
Which made the people start and wonder;
And the tolling of the village bells,
While the solemn music on the air swells.

And the people said, "Prince Henry was a good man,
But now he's laid low in the church of Whippingham."
But when the Grim King his dart does throw,
None can escape death, high or low.

The funeral service was certainly very nice—
Which was by the request of Princess Beatrice—
Which was the rendering of Sullivan's anthem, "Brother,
   before us thou art gone"—
I hope unto thy heavenly home.

No Doubt the Princess Beatrice will mourn for him—
But to mourn for the dead it is a sin!
Therefore I hope God will comfort her alway,
And watch o'er her children night and day.

Prince Henry was a God-fearing man—
And to deny it few people can—
And very kind to his children dear,
And for the loss of him they will drop a tear.

His relatives covered the coffin lid with wreaths of flowers,
While adown their cheeks flowed tears in showers.
Then the service concluded with "Christ will gather His
   own";
And each one left with a sad heart and went home.

THE BURNING OF THE PEOPLE'S VARIETY THEATRE, ABERDEEN

'Twas in the year of 1896, and on the 30th of September,
Which many people in Aberdeen will long remember;
The burning of the People's Variety Theatre, in Bridge
   Place,
Because the fire spread like lightning at a rapid pace.

The fire broke out on the stage, about eight o'clock,
Which gave to the audience a very fearful shock;
Then a stampede ensued, and a rush was made pell-mell,
And in the crush, trying to get out, many people fell.

The stage flies took fire owing to the gas
Not having room enough by them to pass;
And with his jacket Mr. Macaulay tried to put out the
    flame,
But oh! horrible to relate, it was all in vain.

Detective Innes, who was passing at the time of the fire,
Rendered help in every way the audience could desire,
By helping many of them for to get out,
Which was a heroic action, without any doubt.

Oh! it was a pitiful and fearful sight,
To see both old and young struggling with all their might,
For to escape from that merciless fire,
While it roared and mounted higher and higher.

Oh! it was horrible to hear the cries of that surging crowd,
Yelling and crying for "Help! help!" aloud;
While one old woman did fret and frown
Because her clothes were torn off when knocked down.

A lady and gentleman of the Music Hall company, Monti
    & Spry,
Managed to make their escape by climbing up very high,
To an advertisement board, and smashing the glass of the
    fanlight,
And squeezed themselves through with a great fight.

A little boy's leg was fractured while jumping from the
  gallery,
And by doing so he saved his life miraculously;
And every one of the artistes were in a sorry plight,
Because all their properties was burnt on that night.

There were about 400 or 500 people present on that night,
And oh! to them it was a most appalling sight;
When the flames swept the roof at one stroke,
'Twas then that a fearful yell from the audience broke.

And in a short time the interior was one mass of flames,
And nothing but the bare walls now remains;
But thank God it did not occur on Monday night,
Or else it would have been a more pitiable sight.

Because there was an over-crowded audience on Monday
  night.
The theatre was packed in every corner left and right,
Which certainly was a most pleasant sight,
And seemingly each heart was filled with delight.

The courage of Mr. T. Turner was wonderful to behold,
A private in the 92nd Highlanders, he was a hero bold;
Because he cast off his tunic and cap without delay,
And rescued several of the people without dismay.

Yet many were burned and disfigured in the face,
While trying hard to escape from that burning place;
Because with fear and choking smoke
Many of their hearts were almost broke.

132

But accidents will happen both on sea and land,
And the works of the Almighty is hard to understand;
And thank God there's only a few has fallen victims to
the fire,
But I hope they are now in Heaven, amongst the Heavenly
choir.

THE STORMING OF DARGAI HEIGHTS

'Twas on the 20th of November, and in the year of 1897,
That the cheers of the Gordon Highlanders ascended to
heaven,
As they stormed the Dargai heights without delay,
And made the Indian rebels fly in great dismay.

"Men of the Gordon Highlanders," Colonel Mathias said,
"Now, my brave lads, who never were afraid,
Our General says ye must take Dargai heights to-day;
So, forward, and charge them with your bayonets without
dismay!"

Then with a ringing cheer, and at the word of command,
They bounded after their leaders, and made a bold stand;
And, dashing across the open ground with their officers at
their head,
They drove the enemy from their position without any
dread.

In that famous charge it was a most beautiful sight
To see the regimental pipers playing with all their might;
But, alas! one of them was shot through both ankles, and
fell to the ground,
But still he played away while bullets fell on every side
around.

Oh! it must have been a gorgeous sight that day,
To see two thousand Highlanders dressed up in grand
    array,
And to hear the pibroch sounding loud and clear
While the Highlanders rushed upon the foe with a loud
    cheer.

The Gordon Highlanders have gained a lasting fame
Which for ages to come will long remain :
The daring gallantry they displayed at the storming of
    Dargai,
Which will be handed down to posterity.

Methinks I see that gallant and heroic band
When brave Colonel Mathias gave them the command,
As they rushed upon the rebel horde, which was their
    desire,
Without the least fear through a sheet of fire.

Then the rebels fled like frightened sprites,
And the British were left masters of the Dargai heights;
But, alas! brave Captain Robinson was mortally wounded
    and cut down,
And for his loss many tears from his comrades fell to the
    ground.

Success to the Gordon Highlanders wherever they go.
May they always be enabled to conquer the foe;
And may God guard them always in the fight,
And give them always strength to put their enemies to
    flight.

SAVING A TRAIN

A poor old woman lived on the line of the Ohio Railway,
Where the train passed near by night and day:
She was a widow, with only one daughter,
Who lived with her in a log-hut near a deep gorge of
    water.

Which was spanned o'er from ridge to ridge,
By a strong metal railway bridge;
And she supported herself by raising and selling poultry,
Likewise eggs and berries, in great variety.

She often had to walk to the nearest town,
Which was many miles, but she seldom did frown;
And there she sold her basket of produce right quickly,
Then returned home with her heart full of glee.

The train passed by her hut daily to the town.
And the conductor noticed her on the line passing down,
So he gave her a lift, poor soul, many a time,
When he chanced to see her travelling along the line.

The engineman and brakesman to her were very good,
And resolved to help her all they could;
And thought they were not wronging the railway
    company
By giving the old woman a lift when she felt weary.

And, by thinking so, they were quite right,
For soon an accident occurred in the dead of night,
Which filled the old woman's heart with fright,
When she heard the melted torrents of snow descending
    in the night.

Then the flood arose, and the railway bridge gave way
With a fearful crash and plash,—Oh, horror and dismay!
And fell into the seething and yawning gulf below,
Which filled the old woman's heart with woe.

Because in another half-hour the train would be due,
So the poor old woman didn't know what to do;
And the rain fell in a flood, and the wind was howling,
And the heavens above seemed angry and scowling.

And alas! there was no telegraph along the line,
And what could she do to warn the train in time,
Because a light wouldn't live a moment in the rain,
But to save the train she resolved to strain every vein.

Not a moment was to be lost, so to work she went,
And cut the cords of her bed in a moment;
Then shouldered the side-pieces and head-pieces in all,
Then shouted to her daughter to follow as loud as she
    could bawl.

Then they climbed the steep embankment, and there
    fearlessly stood,
And piled their furniture on the line near the roaring
    flood,
And fired the dry combustibles, which blazed up bright,
Throwing its red light along the line a weird-like sight.

Then the old woman tore her red gown from her back,
And tying it to the end of a stick she wasn't slack;
Then ran up the line, waving it in both hands,
While before, with a blazing chair-post, her daughter
    stands.

Then round a curve the red eye of the engine came at last;
Whilst the poor old woman and her daughter stood aghast,
But, thank God, the engine stoppednear the roaring fire,
And the train was saved, as the old woman did desire.

And such an old woman is worth her weight in gold,
For saving the train be it told;
She was a heroine, true and bold,
Which should be written on her tombstone in letters of
    gold.

THE BATTLE OF ATBARA

Ye Sons of Great Britain, pray list to me,
And I'll tell ye of a great victory.
Where the British defeated the Dervishes, without delay,
At the Battle of Atbara, without dismay.

The attack took place, 'twas on the 8th of April, in the
    early morning dawn,
And the British behaved manfully to a man;
And Mahmud's front was raked fearfully, before the
    assault began,
By the disposition of the force under Colonel Long:
Because the cannonading of their guns was very strong.

The main attack was made by General Gatacre's British
    Brigade,
And a heroic display they really made;
And General Macdonald's and General Maxwell's Brigade
    looked very fine,
And the Cameron Highlanders were extended along the
    line.

And behind them came the Lincolnshire Regiment, on the right,
And the Seaforth Highlanders in the centre, 'twas a most gorgeous sight,
And the Warwickshire Regiment were on the left,
And many of the Dervishes' heads by them were cleft.

General Macdonald's Brigade was on the right centre in similar formation,
And the 9th Battalion also in line in front rotation;
Then the whole force arrived about four o'clock,
And each man's courage was as firm as the rock.

At first the march was over a ridge of gravel,
But it didn't impede the noble heroes' travel;
No, they were as steady as when marching in the valley below,
And each man was eager to attack the foe.

And as the sun shone out above the horizon,
The advancing army, with banners flying, came boldly marching on;
The spectacle was really imposing to see,
And a dead silence was observed throughout the whole army.

Then Colonel Murray addressed the Seaforth Highlanders, and said,
"Come now my lads, don't be afraid,
For the news of the victory must be in London to-night,
So ye must charge the enemy with your bayonets, left and right."

General Gatacre also delivered a stirring address,
Which gave courage to the troops, I must confess;
He told the troops to drive the Dervishes into the
    river,
And go right through the zereba, and do not shiver.

Then the artillery on the right opened fire with grapnel
    and percussion shell,
Whereby many of the Dervishes were wounded and fell,
And the cannonading raked the whole of the Dervishes'
    camp, and did great execution,
Which to Mahmud and his followers has been a great
    retribution.

Then the artillery ceased fire, and the bugles sounded the
    advance,
And the Cameron Highlanders at the enemy were eager to
    get a chance;
So the pipers struck up the March of the Cameron Men,
Which reminded them of the ancient Camerons marching
    o'er mountain and glen.

The business of this regiment was to clear the front with
    a rifle fire,
Which to their honour, be it said, was their greatest
    desire;
Then there was a momentary pause until they reached the
    zereba,
Then the Dervishes opened fire on them, but it did not
    them awe.

And with their pipes loudly sounding, and one ringing
   cheer,
Then the Cameron Highlanders soon did the zereba clear,
And right through the Dervish camp they went without
   dismay,
And scattered the Dervishes across the desert, far, far
   away.

Then the victory was complete, and the British gave three
   cheers,
While adown their cheeks flowed burning tears
For the loss of their commanders and comrades who fell
   in the fray,
Which they will remember for many a day.

Captain Urquhart's last words were "never mind me my
   lads, fight on,"
While, no doubt, the Cameron Highlanders felt woe-
   begone
For the loss of their brave captain, who was foremost in
   the field,
Death or glory was his motto, rather than yield.

There have been 4,000 prisoners taken, including Mahmud
   himself,
Who is very fond of dancing girls, likewise drink and pelf;
Besides 3,000 of his followers have been found dead,
And the living are scattered o'er the desert with their
   hearts full of dread.

Long life and prosperity to the British army,
May they always be able to conquer their enemies by land
   and by sea,
May God enable them to put their enemies to flight,
And to annihilate barbarity, and to establish what is right.

BEAUTIFUL BALMERINO

Beautiful Balmerino on the bonnie banks of Tay,
It's a very bonnie spot in the months of June or May;
The scenery there is charming and fascinating to see,
Especially the surroundings of the old Abbey,

Which is situated in the midst of trees on a rugged hill,
Which visitors can view at their own free will;
And the trees and shrubberies are lovely to view,
Especially the trees on each side of the avenue

Which leads up to the Abbey amongst the trees;
And in the summer time it's frequented with bees,
And also crows with their unmusical cry,
Which is a great annoyance to the villagers that live
    near by.

And there in the summer season the mavis sings,
And with her charming notes the woodland rings;
And the sweet-scented zephyrs is borne upon the gale,
Which is most refreshing and invigorating to inhale.

Then there's the stately Castle of Balmerino
Situated in the midst of trees, a magnificent show,
And bordering on the banks o' the silvery Tay,
Where visitors can spend a happy holiday.

As they view the castle and scenery around
It will help to cheer their spirits I'll be bound;
And if they wish to view Wormit Bay
They can walk along the braes o' the silvery Tay.

THE BATTLE OF OMDURMAN

Ye Sons of Great Britain! come join with me
And sing in praise of the gallant British Armie,
That behaved right manfully in the Soudan,
At the great battle of Omdurman.

'Twas in the year of 1898, and on the 2nd of September,
Which the Khalifa and his surviving followers will long
    remember,
Because Sir Herbert Kitchener has annihilated them
    outright,
By the British troops and Soudanese in the Omdurman
    fight.

The Sirdar and his Army left the camp in grand array,
And marched on to Omdurman without delay,
Just as the brigades had reached the crest adjoining the
    Nile,
And became engaged with the enemy in military style.

The Dervishes had re-formed under cover of a rocky
    eminence,
Which to them, no doubt, was a strong defence,
And they were massed together in battle array
Around the black standard of the Khalifa, which made a
    grand display.

But General Maxwell's Soudanese brigade seized the
    eminence in a short time,
And General Macdonald's brigade then joined the firing
    line;
And in ten minutes, long before the attack could be driven
    home,
The flower of the Khalifa's army was almost overthrown.

Still manfully the dusky warriors strove to make headway,
But the Soudanese troops and British swept them back
without dismay,
And their main body were mown down by their deadly
fire—
But still the heroic Dervishes refused to retire.

And defiantly they planted their standards and died by
them,
To their honour be it said, just like brave men;
But at last they retired, with their hearts full of woe,
Leaving the field white with corpses, like a meadow dotted
with snow.

The chief heroes in the fight were the 21st Lancers;
They made a brilliant charge on the enemy with ringing
cheers,
And through the dusky warriors bodies their lances they
did thrust,
Whereby many of them were made to lick the dust.

Then at a quarter past eleven the Sirdar sounded the
advance,
And the remnant of the Dervishes fled, which was their
only chance,
While the cavalry cut off their retreat while they ran;
Then the Sirdar, with the black standard of the Khalifa,
headed for Omdurman.

And when the Khalifa saw his noble army cut down,
With rage and grief he did fret and frown;
Then he spurred his noble steed, and swiftly it ran,
While inwardly to himself he cried, "Catch me if you
can!"

And Mahdism now has received a crushing blow,
For the Khalifa and his followers have met with a complete
  overthrow;
And General Gordon has been avenged, the good Christian,
By the defeat of the Khalifa at the battle of Omdurman.

Now since the Khalifa has been defeated and his rule at
  an end,
Let us thank God that fortunately did send
The brave Sir Herbert Kitchener to conquer that bad man,
The inhuman Khalifa, and his followers at the battle of
  Omdurman.

Success to Sir Herbert Kitchener! he is a great
  commander,
And as skilful in military tactics as the great Alexander,
Because he devised a very wise plan,
And by it has captured the town of Omdurman.

I wish success to the British and Soudanese Army,
May God protect them by land and by sea,
May he enable them always to conquer the foe,
And to establish what's right wherever they go.

THE VILLAGE OF TAYPORT AND ITS SURROUNDINGS

All ye pleasure-seekers, where'er ye be,
I pray ye all be advised by me,
Go and visit Tayport on the banks o' the Tay,
And there ye can spend a pleasant holiday.

The village and its surroundings are magnificent to be
   seen,
And the shops on the High Street are tidy and clean,
And the goods, I'm sure, would please the Queen,
They cannot be surpassed in Edinburgh or Aberdeen.

And the villagers' gardens are lovely to be seen,
There sweet flowers grow and gooseberries green.
And the fragrant air will make you feel gay
While viewing the scenery there on the banks of the Tay.

Scotscraig is an ancient and a most charming spot,
And once seen by visitors will never be forgot.
'Twas there that Archbishop Sharp lived long ago,
And the flower-garden there is a very grand show.

The flower beds there are very beautiful to see,
They surpass the Baxter Park flower beds in Dundee,
And are all enclosed in a round ring,
And there the bee and the butterfly are often on the wing.

Scotscraig farm-house is magnificent to see
With its beautiful rich fields of wheat and barley,
And the farm-house steading is certainly very fine,
And the scenery is charming in the summer time.

The Serpentine Walk is a secluded spot in Scotscraig
   wood,
And to be walking there 'twould do one's heart good.
There the lovers can enjoy themselves in its shady bowers
By telling tales of love to wile away the tedious hours.

There innocent rabbits do sport and play
During the livelong summer day
Amongst the ivy and shrubberies green,
And screened all day from the sun's sheen.

Then, lovers of the picturesque, off and away
To the village of Tayport on the banks o' the Tay,
And ramble through Scotscraig wood,
It will, I'm sure, do your bodies good.

And, as ye walk along the Serpentine Walk,
With each other ye can have a social talk,
And ye will hear the birds singing away,
Which will make your hearts feel light and gay.

And while walking underneath the branches of the trees,
Ye will hear the humming of the bees.
Therefore, pleasure-seekers, make no delay,
But visit Scotscraig wood on a fine summer day.

There visitors can be shaded from the sun in the summer
    time,
While walking along the secluded Serpentine,
By the spreading branches of the big trees,
Or from the undergrowth ivy, if they please.

Do not forget to visit the old Tower,
Where Archbishop Sharp spent many an hour,
Viewing the beautiful scenery for miles away
Along the bonnie banks o' the silvery Tay.

THE BLIND GIRL

Kind Christians, pray list to me,
And I'll relate a sad story,
Concerning a little blind girl, only nine years of age,
Who lived with her father in a lonely cottage.

Poor girl, she had never seen the blessed light of day,
Nor the beautiful fields of corn and hay,
Nor the sparrows, that lifted their heads at early morn
To bright Sol that does the hills adorn.

And near the cottage door there was an elm tree;
But that stunted elm tree she never did see,
Yet her little heart sometimes felt gay
As she listened to the thrushes that warbled the live-long
    day.

And she would talk to the wren when alone,
And to the wren she would her loneliness bemoan,
And say, "Dear little wren, come again to-morrow;
Now be sure and come, your singing will chase away my
    sorrow."

She was motherless, but she had a drunken father,
Who in his savage moods drank all he could gather,
And would often cruelly beat her until she would cry,
"Dear father, if you beat me I will surely die."

She spent the days in getting ready her father's food,
Which was truly for her drunken father's good;
But one night he came home, reeling drunk,
And the poor child's heart with fear sunk;

And he cried, "You were at the door when I came up the
  lane;
Take that, you good-for-nothing slut; you're to blame
For not having my supper ready; you will find
That's no excuse, Sarah, because you are blind."

And with a stick he struck her as he spoke
Across the shoulders, until the stick almost broke;
Crying aloud, "I'll teach you better, you little sneak;"
And with the beating, Sarah's heart was like to break.

Poor little Sarah had never seen the snow;
She knew it was beautiful white, some children told her so;
And in December, when the snow began to fall,
She would go to the door and make a snowball.

One day she'd been very cheerless and alone,
Poor child, and so cold, almost chilled to the bone;
For her father had spent his wages in drink,
And for want of fire she was almost at death's brink.

Her face was pinched with hunger but she never
  complained,
And her little feet with cold were chilblained,
And her father that day had not come home for dinner,
And the dull grey sky was all of a shimmer.

So poor Sarah was very sick when her father came home;
So bad, little dear, that she did sigh and moan,
And when her father saw her in bed
He was heart-stricken with fear and dread.

So within a few days poor Sarah did die,
And for the loss of Sarah the drunken father did cry,
So the loss of his child soon converted him
From drinking either whisky, rum, or gin.

WRECK OF THE STEAMER MOHEGAN

Good people of high and low degree,
I pray ye all to list to me,
And I'll relate a terrible tale of the sea
Concerning the unfortunate steamer, Mohegan,
That against the Manacles Rocks, ran.

'Twas on Friday, the 14th of October, in the year of
  ninety-eight,
Which alas! must have been a dreadful sight;
She sailed out of the river Thames on Thursday,
While the hearts of the passengers felt light and gay.

And on board there were 133 passengers and crew,
And each one happier than another seemingly to view;
When suddenly the ship received some terrible shocks,
Until at last she ran against the Manacles Rocks.

Dinner was just over when the shock took place,
Which caused fear to be depicted in every face;
Because the ship was ripped open, and the water rushed in,
It was most dreadful to hear, it much such a terrific din.

Then the cries of children and women did rend the air,
And in despair many of them tore their hair
As they clung to their babies in wild despair,
While come of them cried—'Oh, God, do Thou my babies
  spare!'

The disaster occurred between seven and eight o'clock at
  night,
Which caused some of the passengers to faint with fright;
As she struck on the Manacles Rocks between Falmouth
  and Lizard Head,
Which filled many of the passengers' hearts with dread.

Then the scene that followed was awful to behold,
As the captain hurried to the bridge like a hero bold;
And the seamen rushed manfully to their posts,
While many of the passengers with fear looked as pale as
  ghosts.

And the poor women and children were chilled to the
  heart,
And crying aloud for their husbands to come and take
  their part;
While the officers and crew did their duty manfully,
By launching the boats immediately into the sea.

Then lifebelts were tied round the women and children
By the brave officers and gallant seamen;
While the storm fiend did laugh and angry did roar,
When he saw the boats filled with passengers going
  towards the shore.

One of the boats, alas! unfortunately was swamped,
Which caused the officers and seamens' courage to be a
  little damped;
But they were thankful the other boats got safely away,
And tried hard to save the passengers without dismay.

Then a shriek of despair arose as the ship is sinking
  beneath the wave,
While some of the passengers cried to God their lives to
  save;
But the angry waves buffetted the breath out of them,
Alas, poor sickly children, also women and men.

Oh, heaven, it was most heartrending to see
A little girl crying and imploring most piteously,
For some one to save her as she didn't want to die,
But, alas, no one seemed to hear her agonizing cry.

For God's sake, boys, get clear, if ye can,
Were the captain's last words spoken like a brave man;
Then he and the officers sank with the ship in the briny
  deep,
Oh what a pitiful sight, 'tis enough to make one weep.

Oh think of the passengers that have been tempest
  tossed,
Besides, 100 souls and more, that have been lost;
Also, think of the mariner while on the briny deep,
And pray to God to protect him at night before ye sleep.

THE HERO OF RORKE'S DRIFT

Twas at the camp of Rorke's Drift, and at tea-time,
And busily engaged in culinary operations was a private
  of the line;
But suddenly he paused, for he heard a clattering din,
When instantly two men on horseback drew rein beside
  him.

'New's from the front!" said one, "Awful news!" said the other,
"Of which, we are afraid, will put us to great bother,
For the black Zulus are coming, and for our blood doth thirst,"
"And the force is cut up to pieces!" shouted the first.

"We're dead beat," said both, "but we've got to go on,"
And on they rode both, looking very woebegone;
Then Henry Hook put all thought of cooking out of his mind,
For he was surrounded with danger on every side he did find.

He was a private of the South Wales Borderers, Henry Hook,
Also a brave soldier, and an hospital cook;
A soldier of the Queen, who was always ready to obey,
And willing to serve God by night and day.

Then away to the Camp he ran, with his mind all in a shiver,
Shouting, "The force is cut up, sir, on the other side of the river!"
Which caused the officer in command with fear to quiver,
When Henry Hook the news to him did deliver.

Then Henry Hook saluted, and immediately retired,
And with courage undaunted his soul was fired,
And the cry rang out wildly, "The Zulus are coming!"
Then the alarm drums were instantly set a-drumming.

Then "Fall in! Fall in!" the commanders did cry,
And the men mustered out, ready to do and to die,
As British soldiers are always ready to do,
But, alas, on this occasion their numbers were but few.

They were only eighty in number, that brave British band,
And brave Lieutenant Broomhead did them command;
He gave orders to erect barricades without delay,
"It's the only plan I can see, men, to drive four thousand
   savages away."

Then the mealie bags and biscuit boxes were brought out,
And the breastwork was made quickly without fear or
   doubt,
And barely was it finished when some one cried in dismay,
"There's the Zulus coming just about twelve hundred
   yards away."

Methinks I see the noble hero, Henry Hook,
Because like a destroying angel he did look,
As he stood at the hospital entrance defending the patients
   there,
Bayoneting the Zulus, while their cries rent the air,
As they strove hard the hospital to enter in,
But he murdered them in scores, and thought it no sin.

In one of the hospital rooms was stationed Henry Hook,
And every inch a hero he did look,
Standing at his loophole he watched the Zulus come,
All shouting, and yelling, and at a quick run.

On they came, a countless host of savages with a rush,
But the gallant little band soon did their courage crush,
But the cool man Henry Hook at his post began to fire,
And in a short time those maddened brutes were forced to
  retire.

Still on came the savages into the barricade,
And still they were driven back, but undismayed.
Again they came into the barricade, yet they were driven
  back,
While darkness fell swift across the sun, dism al and black.

Then into the hospital the savages forced their way,
And in a moment they set fire to it without dismay,
Then Henry Hook flew to assist the patients in the ward,
And the fighting there was fearful and hard.

With yell and shriek the Zulus rushed to the attack,
But for the sixth time they were driven back
By the brave British band, and Henry Hook,
Who was a brave soldier, surgeon, and hospital cook.

And when Lord Chelmsford heard of the victory that day,
He sent for Henry Hook without delay,
And they took the private before the commander,
And with his braces down, and without his coat, in battle
  array grandeur.

Then Lord Chelmsford said, "Henry Hook, give me your
  hand,
For your conduct to day has been hereoic and grand,
And without your assistance to-day we'd been at a loss,
And for your heroic behaviour you shall receive the
  Victoria Cross."

BEAUTIFUL EDINBURGH

Beautiful city of Edinburgh, most wonderful to be seen,
With your ancient palace of Holyrood and Queen's Park
  Green,
And your big, magnificent, elegant New College,
Where people from all nations can be taught knowledge.

The New College of Edinburgh is certainly very grand
Which I consider to be an honour to fair Scotland,
Because it's the biggest in the world, without any doubt,
And is most beautiful in the inside as well as out.

And the Castle is wonderful to look upon,
Which has withstood many angry tempests in years
  bygone;
And the rock it's built upon is rugged and lovely to be
  seen
When the shrubberies surrounding it are blown full green.

Morningside is lovely and charming to be seen;
The gardens there are rich with flowers and shrubberies
  green
And sweet scented perfumes fill the air,
Emanating from the sweet flowers and beautiful plants
  there.

And as for Braidhill, it's a very romantic spot,
But a fine place to visit when the weather is hot;
There the air is nice and cool, which will help to drive
  away sorrow
When ye view from its summit the beautiful city of
  Edinburgh.

And as for the statues, they are very grand—
They cannot be surpassed in any foreign land;
And the scenery is attractive and fascinating to the eye,
And arrests the attention of tourists as they pass by.

Lord Melville's Monument is most elegant to be seen,
Which is situated in St. Andrew's Square, amongst
   shrubberies green,
Which seems most gorgeous to the eye,
Because it is towering so very high.

The Prince Albert Consort Statue looks very grand,
Especially the granite blocks whereon it doth stand,
Which is admired by all tourists as they pass by,
Because the big granite blocks seem magnificent to the eye.

Princes Street West End Garden is fascinating to be seen,
With its beautiful big trees and shrubberies green,
And its magnificent water fountain in the valley below
Helps to drive away from the tourist all care and woe.

The Castle Hotel is elegant and grand,
And students visit it from every foreign land,
And the students of Edinburgh often call there
To rest and have luncheon, at a very cheap fare.

Queen Street Garden seems charming to the eye,
And a great boon it is to the tenantry near by,
As they walk along the grand gravel walks near there,
Amongst the big trees and shrubberies, and inhale pure air.

Then, all ye tourists, be advised by me,
Beautiful Edinburgh ye ought to go and see.
It's the only city I know of where ye can wile away the time
By viewing its lovely scenery and statues fine.

Magnificent city of Edinburgh, I must conclude my muse,
But to write in praise of thee I cannot refuse.
I will tell the world boldly without dismay
You have the biggest college in the world at the present
     day.

Of all the cities in the world, Edinburgh for me;
For no matter where I look, some lovely spot I see;
And for picturesque scenery unrivalled you do stand.
Therefore I pronounce you to be the Pride of Fair
     Scotland.

WOMEN'S SUFFRAGE

Fellow men! why should the lords try to despise
And prohibit women from having the benefit of the
     parliamentary Franchise ?
When they pay the same taxes as you and me,
I consider they ought to have the same liberty.

And I consider if they are not allowed the same liberty,
From taxation every one of them should be set free;
And if they are not, it is really very unfair,
And an act of injustice I most solemnly declare.

Women, farmers, have no protection as the law now
    stands;
And many of them have lost their property and lands,
And have been turned out of their beautiful farms
By the unjust laws of the land and the sheriffs' alarms.

And in my opinion, such treatment is very cruel;
And fair play, 'tis said, is a precious jewel;
But such treatment causes women to fret and to dote,
Because they are deprived of the parliamentary Franchise
    vote.

In my opinion, what a man pays for he certainly should
    get;
And if he does not, he will certainly fret;
And why wouldn't women do the very same ?
Therefore, to demand the parliamentary Franchise they
    are not to blame.

Therefore let them gather, and demand the parliamentary
    Franchise;
And I'm sure no reasonable man will their actions despise,
For trying to obtain the privileges most unjustly withheld
    from them;
Which Mr. Gladstone will certainly encourage and never
    condemn.

And as for the working women, many are driven to the
    point of starvation,
All through the tendency of the legislation;
Besides, upon members of parliament they have no claim
As a deputation, which is a very great shame.

Yes, the Home Secretary of the present day,
Against working women's deputations, has always said—
  nay;
Because they haven't got the parliamentary Franchise,
That is the reason why he does them despise.

And that, in my opinion, is really very unjust;
But the time is not far distant, I most earnestly trust,
When women will have a parliamentary vote,
And many of them, I hope, will wear a better petticoat.

And I hope that God will aid them in this enterprise,
And enable them to obtain the parliamentary Franchise;
And rally together, and make a bold stand,
And demand the parliamentary Franchise throughout
  Scotland.

And do not rest day nor night—
Because your demands are only right
In the eyes of reasonable men, and God's eyesight;
And Heaven, I'm sure, will defend the right.

Therefore go on brave women! and never fear,
Although your case may seem dark and drear,
And put your trust in God, for He is strong;
And ye will gain the parliamentary Franchise before very
  long.

LORD ROBERTS' TRIUMPHAL ENTRY INTO PRETORIA

'Twas in the year of 1900, and on the 5th of June,
Lord Roberts entered Pretoria in the afternoon;
His triumphal entry was magnificent to see,
The British Army marching behind him fearlessly.

With their beautiful banners unfurled to the breeze,
But the scene didn't the Boers please;
And they immediately made some show of fight,
But at the charge of the bayonet they were put to flight.

The troops, by the people, were received with loud cheers,
While many of them through joy shed joyous tears;
Because Lord Roberts from bondage had set them free,
Which made them dance and sing with glee.

Lord Roberts' march into Pretoria was inspiring to see,
It is reckoned one of the greatest achievements in our
    military history;
Because the Boers were watching him in front and behind,
But he scattered them like chaff before the wind.

Oh! it was a most beautiful and inspiring sight
To see the British bayonets glittering in the sunlight,
Whilst the bands played "See the conquering hero comes,"
While the people in ecstasy towards them run.

The British marched into Pretoria like the rushing tide,
And the Boers around Pretoria there no longer could abide,
Because the British at the charge of the bayonet made them
    run with fear,
And fly from Pretoria just like wild dear.

Then Lord Roberts cried, "Pull down the Transvaal Flag,
And hoist the Union Jack instead of the Transvaal rag;
And shout 'Britannia for ever,' and 'Long live our Queen,'
For she is the noblest Queen the world has ever seen."

Then the Union Jack was hoisted and unfurled to the breeze,
Which certainly did the Boers displease,
When they saw the Union Jack flying o'er their capital,
The sight thereof amazed them, and did them appall.

And when old Kruger saw Lord Roberts he shook with
   fright,
Then he immediately disguised himself and took to flight,
Leaving his poor wife in Pretoria behind,
But the British troops have treated her very kind.

Now let us all thank Lord Roberts for his great bravery,
Who has gained for the people of Pretoria their liberty,
By his skillful tactics and great generalship, be it told,
And the courage of his soldiers, who fought like lions bold.

Lord Roberts is a brave man, be it said,
Who never was the least afraid
To defend his Queen and country when called upon;
And by his valorous deeds great battles he has won.

Then success to Lord Roberts and the British Army,
May God protect them by land and by sea;
And enable them always to conquer the Boers,
And beat all foreign foes from our shores.

A TRIBUTE TO MR J. GRAHAM HENDERSON, THE WORLD'S FAIR JUDGE

Thrice welcome home to Hawick, Mr J. Graham Henderson,
For by your Scotch tweeds a great honour you have won;
By exhibiting your beautiful tweeds at the World's Fair
You have been elected judge of Australian and American
   wools while there.

You had to pass a strict examination on the wool trade,
But you have been victorious, and not the least afraid,
And has been made judge of wools by Sir Henry Truman
  Good,
And was thanked by Sir Henry where he stood.

You have been asked by Sir Henry to lecture on wools
  there,
And you have consented to do so, which made your
  audience stare
When you let them see the difference betwixt good wool
  and bad;
You'll be sure to gain fresh honours, they will feel so glad.

To think they have found a clever man indeed,
That knows good wool and how to manufacture Scotch
  tweed,
I wish you success for many a long day,
Because your Scotch tweeds are the best, I venture to say.

May you always be prosperous wherever you go,
Always gaining fresh friends, but never a foe,
Because you are good and a very clever man,
And to gainsay it there's few people can.

THE WRECK OF THE COLUMBINE

Kind Christians, all pay attention to me,
And Miss Mouat's sufferings I'll relate to ye;
While on board the Columbine, on the merciless sea,
Tossing about in the darkness of night in the storm
  helplessly.

She left her home (Scatness), on Saturday morning, bound
   for Lerwick,
Thinking to get cured by a man she knew, as she was very
   sick;
But for eight days she was tossed about on the stormy main,
By a severe storm of wind, hail, and rain.

The waves washed o'er the little craft, and the wind
   loudly roared,
And the Skipper, by a big wave, was washed overboard;
Then the crew launched the small boat on the stormy
   main,
Thinking to rescue the Skipper, but it was all in vain.

Nevertheless, the crew struggled hard his life to save,
But alas! the Skipper sank, and found a watery grave;
And the white crested waves madly did roar,
Still the crew, thank God, landed safe on shore.

As soon as Miss Mouat found she was alone,
Her mind became absorbed about her friends at home;
As her terrible situation presented itself to her mind,
And her native place being quickly left far behind.

And as the big waves lashed the deck with fearful shocks,
Miss Mouat thought the vessel had struck upon a reef of
   rocks;
And she thought the crew had gone to get help from land,
While she held to a rope fastened to the cabin roof by her
   right hand.

And there the poor creature was in danger of being thrown
to the floor,
Whilst the heavy showers of spray were blown against the
cabin door,
And the loosened sail was reduced to tatters and flapping
with the wind,
And the noise thereof caused strange fears to arise in her
mind.

And after some hours of darkness had set in,
The table capsized with a lurch of the sea which made a
fearful din,
Which helped to put the poor creature in a terrible fright,
To hear the drawers of the table rolling about all the night.

And there the noble heroine sat looking very woe-begone,
With hands uplifted to God making her moan,
Praying to God above to send her relief,
While in frantic screams she gave vent to her pent up grief.

And loud and earnestly to God the noble heroine did cry,
And the poor invalid's bosom heaved many a sigh;
Oh! heaven, hard was the fate of this woman of sixty years
of age,
Tossing about on the briny deep, while the storm fiend did
rage.

Oh! think of the poor soul crouched in the cabin below,
With her heart full of fear, cold, hunger, and woe,
And the pitiless storm of rain, hail, and snow,
Tossing about her tiny craft to and fro.

And when the morning came she felt very sick,
And she expected the voyage would be about three hours
    to Lerwick,
And her stock of provisions was but very small,
Only two half-penny biscuits and a quart bottle of milk in
    all

Still the heavy snow kept falling, and the sky was
    obscured,
And on Sabbath morning she made her first meal on
    board,
And this she confined to a little drop of milk and half a
    biscuit,
Which she wisely considered was most fit.

And to the rope fastened to the cabin roof she still held on
Until her hands began to blister, and she felt woe-begone,
But by standing on a chest she could look out of the
    hatchway,
And spend a little time in casting her eyes o'er the sea
    each day.

When Wednesday morning came the weather was very
    fine,
And the sun in the heavens brightly did shine,
And continued so all the live long day;
Then Miss Mouat guessed that land to the norward lay.

Then the poor creature sat down to her last meal on board,
And with heartfelt thanks she praised the Lord;
But when Thursday morning came no more food could be
    had,
Then she mounted a box about seven o'clock while her heart
    felt sad.

And she took her usual gaze o'er the sea with a wistful eye,
Hoping that some passing vessel she might descry,
And to the westward she espied a bright red light,
But as the little craft passed on it vanished from her sight.

But alas; no vessel could she see around anywhere,
And at last the poor soul began to despair,
And there the lonely woman sat looking out to the heavens
above,
Praying to God for succour with her heart full of love.

At last the Columbine began to strike on submerged rocks,
And with the rise and fall of the sea she received some
dreadful shocks,
And notwithstanding that the vessel was still rolling
among the rocks,
Still the noble heroine contrived once more to raise herself
upon the box.

Still the Columbine sped on, and ran upon a shingly
beach,
And at last the Island of Lepsoe, Miss Mouat did reach,
And she was kindly treated by the inhabitants in everyway
that's grand,
And conveyed to Aalesund and there taking steamer to fair
England.

BALMORAL CASTLE

Beautiful Balmoral Castle,
   Most handsome to be seen,
Highland home of the Empress of India,
   Great Britain's Queen.

Your woods and waters and
   Mountains high are most
Beautiful to see,
   Near by Balmoral Castle
And the dark river Dee.

Then there's the hill of Cairngorm
   To be seen from afar,
And the beautiful heathery hills
   Of dark Lochnagar,
And the handsome little village—
   The Castleton o' Braemar—
Which is most beautiful to see,
   Near by Balmoral Castle
And the dark river Dee.

Then there's the handsome little church
   Of Crathie—most beautiful to be seen;
And the Queen goes there on Sunday
   To hear the Word of God
Most solemn and serene,
   Which is most beautiful to see,
Nor far from Balmoral Castle
   And the dark river Dee.

Then, when she finds herself
   At leisure, she goes for to see
Her old female acquaintances
   That lives on the river Dee,
And reads the Bible unto them,
   Which is most beautiful to see,
Near by Balmoral Castle
   And the dark river Dee.

Beautiful Balmoral Castle!
    In the summer season of the year
The Queen comes to reside in thee,
    Her spirits for to cheer,
And to see her hiland deer,
    And in the green woods to roam
And admire the hiland cataracts,
    With their misty foam,
Which is most beautiful to see,
    Near by Balmoral Castle
And the dark river Dee.

Beautiful Balmoral Castle,
    With your green swards and flowers fair,
Thee Queen of great Britain
    Is always welcome there;
For they young and they old
    Tries to do for her all they can,
And they faithful Highlanders there
    Will protect her to a man,
Which is most beautiful to see,
    Near by Balmoral Castle
And thee dark river Dee.

A NEW TEMPERANCE POEM, IN MEMORY OF MY DEPARTED PARENTS, WHO WERE SOBER LIVING & GOD FEARING PEOPLE

My parents were sober living, and often did pray,
For their family to abstain from intoxicating drink alway;
Because they knew it would lead them astray,
Which no God fearing man will dare to gainsay.

Some people do say that God made strong drink,
But he is not so cruel I think;
To lay a stumbling block in his children's way,
And then punish them for going astray.

No! God has more love for his children, than mere man.
To make strong drink their souls to damn;
His love is more boundless than mere man's by far,
And to say not it would be an unequal par.

A man that truly loves his family wont allow them to
    drink,
Because he knows seldom about God they will think,
Besides he knows it will destroy their intellect,
And cause them to hold their parents in disrespect.

Strong drink makes the people commit all sorts of evil,
And must have been made by the Devil
For to make them quarrel, murder, steal, and fight,
And prevent them from doing what is right.

The Devil delights in leading the people astray,
So that he may fill his kingdom with them without delay;
It is the greatest pleasure he can really find,
To be the enemy of all mankind.

The Devil delights in breeding family strife,
Especially betwixt man and wife;
And if the husband comes home drunk at night,
He laughs and crys, ha! ha! what a beautiful sight.

And if the husband asks his supper when he comes in,
The poor wife must instantly find it for him;
And if she cannot find it, he will curse and frown,
And very likely knock his loving wife down.

Then the children will scream aloud,
And the Devil no doubt will feel very proud,
If he can get the children to leave their own fireside,
And to tell their drunken father, they won't with him
   reside.

Strong drink will cause the gambler to rob and kill his
   brother,
Aye! also his father and his mother,
All for the sake of getting money to gamble,
Likewise to drink, cheat, and wrangle.

And when the burglar wants to do his work very handy,
He plies himself with a glass of Whisky, Rum, or Brandy,
To give himself courage to rob and kill,
And innocent people's blood to spill.

Whereas if he couldn't get Whisky, Rum, or Brandy,
He wouldn't do his work so handy;
Therefore, in that respect let strong drink be abolished in
   time,
And that will cause a great decrease in crime.

Therefore, for this sufficient reason remove it from
   society,
For seldom burglary is committed in a state of sobriety;
And I earnestly entreat ye all to join with heart and hand,
And to help to chase away the Demon drink from bonnie
   Scotland.

I beseech ye all to kneel down and pray,
And implore God to take it away;
Then this world would be a heaven, whereas it is a hell,
And the people would have more peace in it to dwell

Ah! pity the sorrows of a poor poet, when unable to pay
   his rent;
And help him to pay it, and he will feel content.

DAVID WINTER AND SON LTD., PRINTERS, DUNDEE